IRVING BERLIN'S
SHOW BUSINESS

Broadway

Hollywood

America

HARRY N. ABRAMS, INC., PUBLISHERS

IRVING BERLIN'S
SHOW BUSINESS

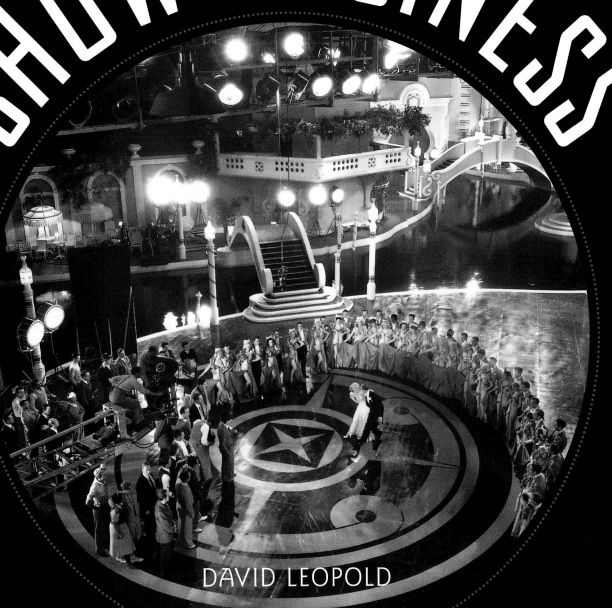

DAVID LEOPOLD

CONTENTS

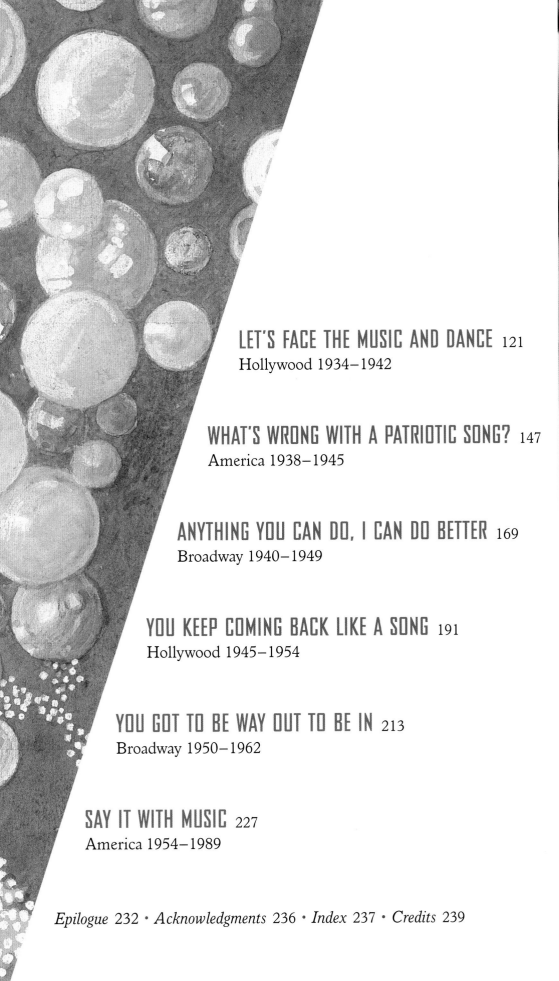

INTRODUCTION

Irving Berlin loved the world of show business. He spent his life in the thick of it, and you can find elements of it in virtually all of his stage and film work. His bible was *Variety*, and his early idol and mentor was George M. Cohan, the man who practically invented show business in America. "He was the guy I tried to write like," said Berlin. "He supplied us with the songs we sang in the so-called saloons—and they were saloons—and what we sang went out all through America. He was the greatest."

Berlin saw Cohan as a model, and tried not only to live up to his standard, but to do better. Dave Dreyer, who worked with Berlin for years, saw that the songwriter was "motivated by the thought that anything he did had to be better than anything he had ever done. And if possible, better than anyone else had ever done before."

What Berlin did was express feelings and emotions in his words and music that continue to articulate a wide range of experience for millions of listeners, singers, and musicians. His art remains part of our vocabulary because its seeming simplicity contains essential truths of human nature. "Berlin's great secret is that he says exactly what he means," remarked Oscar Hammerstein II, who understood the power of a song. "Sometimes he hits a gigantic line both musically and lyrically—almost Wagnerian in its strength."

Few artists have left the mark on American culture that Irving Berlin has. During his extraordinary long and active career—from 1907 to 1966—Berlin was at the forefront of every form of mass popular culture: sheet music, the Broadway stage, radio, records (he had twenty-six number-one songs), film, and television.

American culture also left its mark on Berlin. He took a variety of ethnic dialects and melodies, the strains of classical music and opera, the roar of the city, the wit of the Algonquin Round Table, the bravado of Broadway, and a larger-than-life Hollywood, and transmuted those elements into his own idiom: songs that speak to and for everyone. In the words of Jerome Kern, Berlin gave "these impressions back to the world,—simplified,—clarified,—glorified."

Though an immigrant himself, Berlin formed an idea of America that was all-inclusive. He transformed religious holidays into national celebrations with his songs "White Christmas" and "Easter Parade." He wrote and performed in morale-boosting shows during both world wars, donating the profits to government organizations.

He also contributed his earnings from the country's unofficial anthem, "God Bless America," raising millions for the Boy and Girl Scouts. His more than twelve hundred songs continue to define what Henry Luce called "the American century."

For Irving Berlin there really was no business like show business. Early on he learned how to "sell" a song, and never lost his enthusiasm for it. He understood the commerce that goes hand in hand with creativity, and without any formal training in either music or business, became a genius at both.

After his earliest efforts, he did not work with a collaborator, unlike most of his songwriting contemporaries. Berlin was also unique in that he published his own music for almost his entire six-decade career. Berlin also took an active role in producing his own Broadway shows; he owned his own theater; and he was the first songwriter in Hollywood to get a percentage of a film's gross. A famous insomniac, he frequently took care of business during the day and wrote songs at night. Berlin felt that one could not write a "popular song"; it had to become popular because of the sheer number of people who bought the sheet music, recording, and/or tickets. Giving the people what they wanted was his uncanny talent.

Berlin also understood the "show" of show business. He worked with the top designers on Broadway and in Hollywood, and their art was almost as memorable as his words and music. Berlin's career also coincided with a golden age of illustration. Audiences often received their first glimpses of Berlin's latest triumph through caricatures, drawings, and paintings in publications across the country.

The goal of this book is to show Berlin's career as he and his audiences saw it, from the lavishly illustrated sheet music covers of his first songs to the image of Marilyn Monroe delivering a sultry version of "Heat Wave" in Berlin's final film. This compendium of Berlin iconography demonstrates that the popularity of Berlin's songs, stage shows, and films allowed his visual legacy to seep into the national consciousness almost as much as his music did.

I have not attempted to analyze Berlin's music or lyrics to any great extent. The songs really do speak for themselves. Nor does space allow for a complete history of every aspect of his career. What I present here are text and pictures that bear witness to Berlin's influence on American popular culture, particularly the transition of songs from sheet music to recordings, from vaudeville to revues to the integrated book musical, from silent movies to all-singing ones and from regional favorites to national anthems. I have combed public and private archives to provide a fresh view of Berlin's career, and I have tried to present a lively history of the man and his music. The narrative is arranged under three primary headings: Broadway, Hollywood, and America. Each chapter examines a different aspect of Berlin's career and overlaps with others to reveal the cross-pollination of his work.

It is a shame that this book cannot sing, as Berlin's songs have been my constant companion as I have explored his career. The book may best be enjoyed by cueing up the music, whether from an Edison cylinder or an I-pod, as you look through its pages. But now, as Berlin put it in his famous song, "Let's go on with the show."

Irving Berlin emigrated from Russia to America with his family in 1893, taking up residence in a Lower East Side tenement. He left home at thirteen and started singing in the streets and in saloons to earn money. Soon he was hired as a singing waiter at a notorious dive, where he wrote his first song. Two years later he was a staff writer at an established music publisher. Working day and night, and after many hits, he was made a partner in the firm, which now bore his name. Before the end of his first decade as a songwriter, he opened his own publishing company.

Berlin listened to the world around him. The "hum of the engine, the whirr of the wheels, the explosion of the exhaust" were all incorporated into his music. He told a reporter in 1914 that "the new age demands new music for new action." Berlin clearly loved to write songs and to hear people sing them. In his first decade on Tin Pan Alley, he wrote songs on virtually all the standard themes of the trade, including story songs, paeans to the South, and ethnic comedies. These were sung around the piano in private homes, in vaudeville, and interpolated into Broadway shows. His ceaseless industry would lead him to become the most successful songwriter of all time.

Berlin and his family arrived in a New York that was crowded, noisy, and rapidly changing, as reflected in the painting at right, *The Bowery at Night* by W. Louis Sonntag, Jr., ca. 1895.

AMERICA
1888-1914

Prelude

1888

May 11 Israel Beilin born to cantor Moses Beilin and his wife, Leah (above), in Russia, in what is believed to have been Tyumen, in Western Siberia. He was the youngest of eight children.

1893

The Beilins and seven of their children emigrate to New York on the S.S. *Rhynland*. The family name is changed to Baline. They move first to a basement apartment on Monroe Street on the Lower East Side of Manhattan before settling around the corner on the third floor of a tenement at 330 Cherry Street.

1901–1904

July 21 Fifty-three-year-old Moses Baline dies of chronic bronchitis and atherosclerosis.

1902–1904 Thirteen-year-old Israel works as a "newsie," then a busker. Hired as a chorus boy but soon fired from the Broadway-bound production of *The Show Girl*.

Songwriter/publisher Harry Von Tilzer hires Israel as a song plugger at Tony Pastor's Music Hall, where from the balcony he would "spontaneously" launch into the von Tilzer song featured in an act, as if carried away by its brilliance.

1905–1906

Israel is hired as a singing waiter at the Pelham Café (above) and gains notoriety for devising parody lyrics to popular songs. He earns seven dollars a week and tips by working from eight at night until six in the morning.

1912

January The Ted Snyder Company changes its name to Waterson, Berlin & Snyder, in the wake of "Alexander's Ragtime Band."

February 2 Berlin marries Dorothy Goetz, the sister of sometime collaborator E. Ray Goetz. She dies on July 17 after contracting typhoid during their honeymoon in Cuba.

1913

November 8 Berlin copyrights his first song after Dorothy's death, his first significant ballad, "When I Lost You."

July Berlin writes "The International Rag" the night before he opens in the London musical revue *Hello, Ragtime* at the Hippodrome Theatre.

October 19 The Friars Club gives a dinner in Berlin's honor. Instead of a speech, Berlin sings the comic "What Am I Gonna Do?"

1914

February Berlin becomes a charter member of a new songwriters' organization, ASCAP.

December Berlin opens Irving Berlin, Inc., to publish his theater music. Three years later he opens his own publishing company for all of his music.

1907

Mike Salter orders "Izzy" and pianist Mike Nicholson to write a song to compete with the saloon around the corner where the pianist had written a hit song. The two produce "Marie from Sunny Italy," with Izzy writing the words. It is not a hit, and Izzy claims later to make only thirty-seven cents for his efforts. It does give him a new name: "I. Berlin." Izzy is soon hired at the more upscale saloon Jimmy Kelly's, on Fourteenth Street.

1909

Writes "Dorando," his first hit. It is published by the Ted Snyder Company. Berlin is hired as a staff writer. He publishes several songs, some of which become the most popular of the year, including "Sadie Salome, Go Home," "That Mesmerizing Mendelssohn Tune," and "My Wife's Gone to the Country (Hurrah! Hurrah!)," often collaborating with someone who can play piano and write musical notation.

1910

April Berlin writes his first number-one hit, "Call Me Up Some Rainy Afternoon."

July 10 *Up and Down Broadway* opens at the Casino Theatre on Broadway, featuring Berlin and Ted Snyder performing two new songs. Berlin meets the female lead, Emma Carus, who agrees to sing new Berlin songs when she returns to vaudeville the following spring.

1911

April 17 Emma Carus introduces "Alexander's Ragtime Band" at the American Music Hall in Chicago. The song is a hit and she continues to sing it for the next two months. In May, with an accompanist, Berlin sings it during *The Friars' Frolic of 1911*. He later described his act as, "We sang, did a little dance, and went off with a cartwheel." That summer the song is interpolated into vaudeville acts and Broadway productions. The sheet music sells more than two million copies internationally.

With a pull of a lever, Berlin's transposing piano allowed him to write in other keys, even though he could play only in F sharp.

THIS IS
THE LIFE

In the summer of 1910 Irving Berlin made his only appearance in a Broadway show, performing with his songwriting partner and publisher, Ted Snyder, in an Eddie Foy musical comedy, *Up and Down Broadway*. In the second act Berlin and Snyder "bounded on wearing sweaters, carrying tennis rackets and trying to look as much as possible like two genteel young athletes considerably surprised at finding a piano there in the middle of the garden," according to Berlin biographer Alexander Woollcott. Snyder played while Berlin sang two new songs they had written: an ethnic comedy number, "Sweet Italian Love," and, to capture the ragtime craze, "Oh, That Beautiful Rag." One review described how the two worked "first to get on friendly terms with the audience and then to turn them into a lot of college boys rah-rah-rahing for two men who were perfect strangers to them five minutes before, but who had suddenly become personal friends." They gave five encores and even after the house lights were turned off to proceed with the next scene, they were called back again.

The female lead, Emma Carus, was an established star, an actress, comedienne, dancer, and singer on both Broadway and in vaudeville. She was known for her "coon shouting" and claimed to have "learned the Negro dialect from a colored man, known only to posterity as 'Frog Eyes.'" She was just as successful in exciting her audience with ethnic songs of every conceivable strain. She claimed, "I'm the human dialect cocktail. A little Scotch, considerable Irish, a dash of Dutch, and a great deal of Negro, together with a bit of British." At that time ethnic comedy songs were not considered demeaning, and in the early years of the twentieth century only sentimental ballads were more popular. Vaudeville audiences were often made up of immigrants who were as happy to laugh at their national or racial stereotypes as anyone else. For them, it meant they had become part of the American story.

The Casino Theatre at Broadway and Thirty-ninth Street, where Berlin performed in *Up and Down Broadway*.

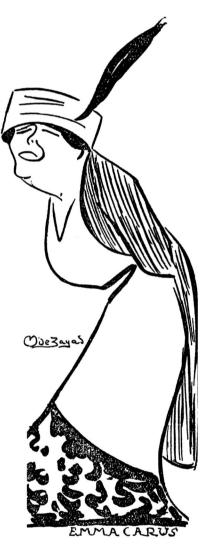

Emma Carus in *Up and Down Broadway*, as caricatured by Marius de Zayas, a contemporary of Alfred Stieglitz.

Vaudeville, a new form of entertainment, had started in Bowery saloons and would eventually establish itself all over the country in the late nineteenth century and into the early twentieth century. A bill (usually) featured eight or more acts, a combination of singers, dancers, comics, and animal acts, each between ten to twenty minutes in length. The audience was predominantly working-class and two-thirds male. The audience for the "legitimate" stage was, by contrast, only 2 percent working-class, and was more evenly divided by gender. "The theaters were small; you could almost touch the actors on stage," one spectator remembered. "Their personalities reached over the footlights; you could see every change of expression; you could hear every word and catch every intonation. There was free movement; no microphones got in the way!"

Emma Carus, ca. 1911, when she first introduced "Alexander's Ragtime Band."

Many of Berlin's early songs were written for vaudeville performers who were friends. "You get very close to people when you work together," remembered Berlin a half century later. "When I was writing songs for Al Jolson, and Fanny Brice, and Bert Williams, we were all very close." These singers could cause a sensation with a song that would make it a success. At the time, when a song was popular, thousands, or even millions, of people purchased the sheet music to play on pianos in their homes. A song's publishers often had a department whose sole job was to circulate new songs to vaudeville performers in hopes that one might catch on with an audience in this manner.

When *Up and Down Broadway* closed on September 17, 1910, Emma Carus left with the understanding that she wanted to add several Berlin songs to her act when she went back to vaudeville. That winter Berlin returned to an instrumental that he had put aside. Just before he left for a

Berlin played a role in Fanny Brice's early success. She scored a hit with "Sadie Salome, Go Home," and in her *Ziegfeld Follies* debut she sang two other Berlin songs.

trip to Palm Beach he remembered the piece and wrote lyrics to it in less than half an hour, intending it to be sent to Carus for her next engagement in April. With its choral invitation of "Come on and hear!," "Alexander's Ragtime Band" would soon start, in Berlin's words, "the heels and shoulders of all America and a good section of Europe to rocking."

He published the song in March 1911, so confident of its success that above the title it was announced "successfully intruduced [sic] by Emma Carus." Carus did not sing the song until mid-April, but Berlin had been right, it was the hit of her performance. Carus brought the song to New York in May, and one reviewer accurately predicted that "In a few days 'Alexander' will be whistled on the streets and played in the cafes. It is the most meritorious addition to the list of popular songs introduced this season. The vivacious comedienne soon had her audience singing the choruses with her and those who did not sing whistled." Soon all of vaudeville, and then Broadway, was singing the song. It attracted more attention than any other song of the decade, and would be the poster child for the entire ragtime craze that swept the country and Europe following its debut. Yet it was not a ragtime song but, in Berlin's words, "a song about ragtime…I didn't originate [ragtime]. Maybe I crystallized it and brought it to people's attention." Nevertheless, with the song's choppy syncopation, the twenty-three-year-old Irving Berlin was crowned the King of Ragtime and feted around the world as a true American voice.

Only ten years earlier, Berlin had left his family on the Lower East Side so that his widowed mother and hardworking brother and sisters would not be burdened with his mouth to feed. As the youngest, he had felt that his meager earnings at a variety of small jobs added little to the family's finances, and until he could bring in his fair share, he

LEFT: "Alexander's Ragtime Band" was a hit in America and Europe, where it came to represent American popular music.

RIGHT: Bert Williams was the most popular comedian, black or white, of the period. Berlin wrote "Woodman, Woodman, Spare that Tree" for him to sing in the *Ziegfeld Follies of 1911*.

"Alexander's Ragtime Band" was so popular in the summer and fall of 1911 that comic strips spoofed its ubiquity.

decided to make it on his own. He slept in flophouses, or sometimes on the streets around the Bowery, the most dangerous section of New York at that time, called the "paradise of the criminal." He was one of more than ten thousand homeless in the region. He first worked as a newsboy, then a busker, singing popular songs in the streets or in saloons for whatever coins were tossed his way. Although not a great singer, he learned how to "sell" a song, and his ballad singing could bring tears to even a hardened drunkard's eyes.

He was befriended by the self-proclaimed Mayor of Chinatown, Chuck Connors, who often took tourists through the dens of iniquity in the Bowery for fun and profit. Connors probably helped Izzy (as he was known then) get a job as a singing waiter at the Pelham Café, one of the area's more colorful watering holes,

Alexander Woollcott described the backroom of the Pelham Café, where Berlin wrote his first song, as "a thieves' Algonquin, a pickpockets' Round Table, a coffee house for the lawless."

owned by Mike Salter, a swarthy Russian whose complexion gave the place another name. As Alexander Woollcott later wrote, "It was not so known on the blotters at Police Headquarters. It was not so known in the gaudier journals when the tearful sorority would seek to lend a dash of local color to some tale of white slavery. It was not spoken as of the Pelham Café in the jargon of the thieves and opium peddlers and street-walkers who rubbed shoulders with the sightseers in the narrow street where it stood.... Everyone called it 'Nigger Mike's.'"

The Pelham Café was a regular stop for criminals, prostitutes, and anyone looking to lose himself in a shot of hard liquor. Working all night, Berlin and his fellow waiters took turns at devising parody lyrics to popular tunes. Often racy, they were just as frequently done in dialects and stereotypes that would shock most audiences today but were enjoyed by the Pelham's patrons. Customers started to forsake the dive when Callahan's, a saloon around the corner, featured a new hit song, "My Mariucci Take a Steamboat," written by their own piano

Chuck Connors (second from right) took uptown society through the Bowery and showed them manufactured scenes of licentiousness and drug use, before taking them to the Pelham Café for local color and a drink.

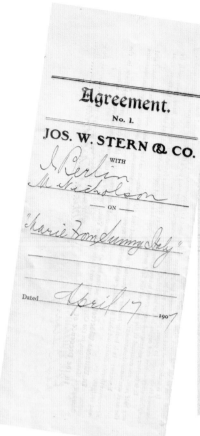

ABOVE: The contract and royalty statement for Berlin's first song, "Marie from Sunny Italy."

BELOW: Berlin idolized Stephen Foster, the nineteenth century's most popular songwriter. He hung this photograph of the composer of "Beautiful Dreamer" and "Oh! Susannah" in his office.

player and waiter. In response, Salter demanded that his staff quickly come up with a song. Berlin worked with the saloon's pianist, Mike Nicholson, on the assignment, with Berlin supplying the words and Nicholson the music. When they had come up with "Marie from Sunny Italy," an Italian-dialect love song, they were chagrined to discover that neither knew how to transcribe their work. Berlin had spent odd moments at the piano picking at melodies in the key of F sharp. It would be another twenty-five years before he could take down a lead sheet, the melodic line of a song.

When the song was finally transcribed, Berlin and Nicholson shopped around Tin Pan Alley, a warren of offices on West Twenty-eighth Street, for a publisher to put out their song. Joseph Stern took a chance on it. Berlin claimed thirty-seven cents was all he ever made on the song, which was not a hit. Stern mistakenly credited the song's lyrics not to Baline but to "I. Berlin," and a new name and personality was born.

Despite the song's failure (Berlin joked that pharmacist and soon-to-be movie producer Joe Schenck bought the only copy), Berlin enjoyed the experience, and less than a year later he had another song published (in which he is credited with both the words and music). Another flop. A third, written three weeks later with Maurice Abrahams, fared no better.

By this time, Salter had fired the budding songwriter for sleeping on the job, and Berlin found himself working in the more upscale Jimmy Kelly's on Union Square. Performers were often customers and one singer asked Berlin for an Italian dialect song. The talk at the time was of the Italian marathon runner Dorando

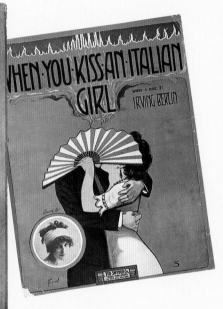

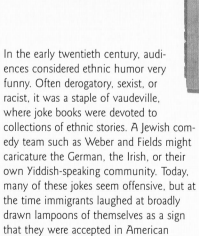

In the early twentieth century, audiences considered ethnic humor very funny. Often derogatory, sexist, or racist, it was a staple of vaudeville, where joke books were devoted to collections of ethnic stories. A Jewish comedy team such as Weber and Fields might caricature the German, the Irish, or their own Yiddish-speaking community. Today, many of these jokes seem offensive, but at the time immigrants laughed at broadly drawn lampoons of themselves as a sign that they were accepted in American society.

Tin Pan Alley produced a flood of ethnic songs, and beginning with his first one, Irving Berlin wrote many during his first decade of songwriting, adding the dialects of his Italian, Irish, German, and Jewish neighbors on the Lower East Side to his musical vocabulary. He also wrote songs featuring black protagonists, many of these, as historian Charles Hamm has pointed out, appreciative numbers that celebrate the music or dance of African Americans.

In the first two decades of Berlin's career, the mark of a successful song was not how often it was played on stage, but how many copies of the sheet music were sold. Everything in a music publishing company was geared to selling as many copies as possible. Many stores had sheet music sections, and some department stores even had a pianist on hand to play songs for potential buyers. Songs were often auditioned for performers before publication in the hope that they would add them to their acts; if they did, the publisher would feature the performer on the cover of the music. In this way, both performer and publisher were able to use each other for self-promotion.

Beyond the buyer's hearing a song performed, the most effective way to sell sheet music was to give it a beautiful cover. The publication of illustrated sheet music in the United States began in the late eighteenth century, but did not

become widespread until the introduction of chromolithography in the mid-nineteenth century. This development coincided with the popularity of pianos in the home after the Civil War. By 1910, nearly thirty million copies of sheet music were being sold every year. With so many pieces of music offered, publishers understood that a good cover was crucial. These years were a golden age of illustration and commercial printing. Publishers used the very best of each to make their covers, many of which are still as vivid today as they were when they were first printed. Before television and radio, the country's shared visual culture included the lavish illustrations found on the music stands and pianos in many homes.

The covers of Berlin's sheet music present important pictorial representations of life in early twentieth-century America. Whether featuring images of soldiers in World War I or the latest women's fashions, Berlin's covers convey a colorful history to us now. The images of performers that appear also give us a backstage pass to the world of vaudeville and the early legitimate stage, bringing to life personalities who live today only as voices on old 78s, or as names in books.

The artists who created the iconic images of Berlin's music worked in relative obscurity. Publishers occasionally had an artist on staff for covers, but just as frequently they worked with an array of freelance artists. The work of John Frew, who created the seminal cover for "Alexander's Ragtime Band"—and who was probably responsible for misspelling "introduced" on the original cover—is part of the Berlin legacy. Frew designed a number of Berlin sheet music covers in the first two decades of the twentieth century, including "My Wife's Gone to the Country, Hurrah! Hurrah!" (opposite, bottom), two covers for "Somebody's Coming to My House," and "They've Got Me Doin' It Now." Considered an eccentric, Frew died penniless in a mental hospital in the 1920s.

Albert W. Barbelle, formally trained in Europe as a painter, was another contributor. Perhaps his best-known Berlin cover is "Oh! How I Hate to Get Up in the Morning." He may have

been picked for the job because he had created the cover for Cohan's "Over There," but he had already supplied covers for such patriotic songs as "Over the Seas Boys," "Let's All Be Americans Now," and "They Were All out of Step but Jim." Barbelle was fashion-conscious, and his designs for songs like "My Sweetie" and "Araby" (opposite) feature stylish portraits of well-dressed women.

Gene Buck, who would gain fame as a lyricist for the Ziegfeld Follies, started his career as an illustrator. He supplied Ted Snyder and Berlin with a number of covers before 1920 including "That Society Bear," "I Want to Be in Dixie," and "Yiddisha Professor."

While many artists created covers for Berlin's sheet music, the go-to guy was E. H. Pfeiffer. A review of more than 250 covers of Berlin's music shows that more than a quarter were created by Pfeiffer. "Sadie Salome, Go Home," "The Ragtime Soldier Man" (above), "Yiddle, on Your Fiddle, Play Some Ragtime," and many other important early Berlin songs featured a Pfeiffer cover. Pfeiffer was a lifelong New Yorker, born in 1868, who designed costume jewelry along with magazine and newspaper illustrations. His most memorable works are his wide array of sheet music covers, whose subjects range from portraits to genre scenes, from animals to automobiles. The visual legacy of Berlin's songs reveals the national consciousness of his time as much as the music itself does.

As the 1920s began, illustrated covers changed. The large format grew smaller. As the Jazz Age took hold, lavish illustrations gave way to a more muted palette and picture style. Now covers featured sleek, Art Deco–inspired designs appropriate for the contemporary fashion, especially for urban settings, rather than profusely pictorial images. Sydney Leff's understated but effective covers often graced Berlin's music in the 1920s and 1930s. He supplied the original designs for the covers of "Blue Skies," "How Deep Is the Ocean?," and "Say It Isn't So."

Beginning in the 1930s, Berlin wrote most of his songs for either Broadway shows or Hollywood films. Covers for that kind of sheet music featured the unsigned designs of either the producer's publicity staff or the studio art departments, bringing an end to the heyday of the illustrated cover. The popularity of Berlin's songs allowed his visual legacy to become part of the national consciousness almost as much as his music did.

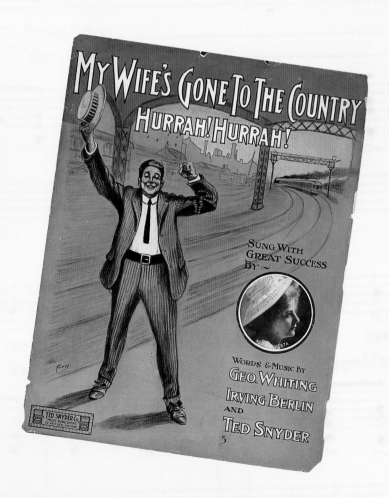

Throughout his career, Berlin embraced new media as a way of bringing his music to a wider audience. In early-twentieth-century America, one popular theater entertainment was the use of illustrated song slides that provided colorful imagery while the house musicians performed a song. Introduced by a picture of the illustrated sheet music cover, the show often ended with a slide of the lyrics to the chorus, so that the audience could sing along. The two pictures shown above are from a sequence that accompanied Berlin's "Yiddle, on Your Fiddle, Play Some Ragtime."

Pietri, who had lost a race at the 1908 London Olympics because of a technicality. Berlin used the idea of the runner as the basis for his song "Dorando." Once he composed the lyrics, he took the song to the Ted Snyder Company to publish it. Snyder's partner, Henry Waterson, liked it and asked how long it would take to write up. Berlin spent an hour with a house arranger and sold the song to the company for twenty-five dollars. It was his first, although moderate, commercial success, sung in vaudeville by Amy Butler.

Waterson saw promise in the young man and offered him a job as a staff lyricist. Soon the songs began to pour out. A month later he scored another, even bigger, hit with a Jewish dialect song, "Sadie Salome, Go Home," a comic song about a man who goes to see the risqué opera *Salome* only to discover that his own sweetheart is singing the title role. Again, Berlin had drawn on current events, as the Met's controversial production of Strauss's opera *Salome,* with its Dance of the Seven Veils, had been closed after one performance in response to public outrage.

Six weeks later Berlin topped that success with "My Wife's Gone to the Country, Hurrah! Hurrah!" This was a major hit, and Berlin was asked to write scores of additional verses for the paper he had once sold on the streets, *The Evening Journal.* As a lyricist working with different composers, he was the constant in all of these successes, and he may have contributed much to the music as well. He often started with a title or an idea, and gradually worked up some verses and picked out a melody in the key of F sharp. Once he felt he had something, he would ask a trained musician to take it down. Soon, however, Berlin bought a transposing piano, which had a lever under its keyboard that allowed him to shift into other

keys. He often referred to it as "my Buick." A fixture in Tin Pan Alley, the transposing piano soon became part of the Berlin legend. Still working on the black keys in F sharp, Berlin would soon hire a musical secretary to transcribe what he had worked out on his piano.

Often writing as many as five songs a week, Berlin published only a handful, putting others into his files, or his "trunk," as he called it. Some surfaced again; many others did not. But he got his published songs out quickly. With so many successes behind him, he had vaudeville performers clamoring for his songs.

ABOVE RIGHT: Berlin must have been amused when stories attesting to the corrupting influence of ragtime were published around the country, much as articles later would decry rock 'n' roll. The article shown above, from an unknown newspaper, was found in one of his scrapbooks.

ABOVE LEFT: A sheet music display, ca. 1913.

Irving and Dorothy Berlin honeymooning in Cuba in February 1912. Dorothy caught typhoid there; she died five months later.

In early 1912, smitten with the spirited Dorothy Goetz, Berlin asked the sister of his close friend and sometime collaborator, E. Ray Goetz, to marry him. To reporters he said that she gave him something to think about other than success and work. The newlyweds honeymooned in Cuba and returned to a new apartment on Seventy-second Street and Riverside Drive. But soon Dorothy became ill. Berlin brought in the best doctors, but she did not get better. In an age before antibiotics, she died only five months after their marriage from a combination of pneumonia and typhoid fever, which she had caught in Cuba.

Berlin was devastated. His brother-in-law first took him to Europe, and on returning encouraged Berlin to channel his pain into song. Berlin was skeptical. He saw songwriting as a business. He did not want to commercialize his personal loss. When he found a love song he had put aside, a welter of emotion came through in a poignant ballad, "When I Lost You," that was unlike anything he had written before. The song, surprisingly, became a hit, second in popularity only to "Alexander's Ragtime Band." Although he would not immediately write another similar song, over the years he would write a string of ballads that are among his greatest works.

For Berlin, a vaudeville performance provided an instant reaction from the audience, letting him know whether the piece was good or not. Berlin was not out to impress critics or reviewers; he wanted the people in the seats to like his music and, more important, to sing it. They were the ones who bought sheet music. Berlin's songs for the variety stage coincided with the genre's heyday, and he worked with the greatest singers in vaudeville: Nora Bayes, Belle Baker, Al Jolson, Sam Bernard, Elsie Janis, Stella Mayhew, and Fritzi Scheff. Having conquered vaudeville and the sheet music business, Berlin had only one place left to go: uptown to Broadway.

The Friars Club's ranks included the top vaudeville and burlesque performers, a group that understood show business. George M. Cohan made Berlin a member in 1911. In 1913, they honored the songwriter with a "roast," with Cohan presiding over the evening. Berlin's shyness precluded a speech, but he composed a song, "What Am I Gonna Do?," which introduced a selection of his own songs.

In the age before radio, television, and film, the legitimacy of the Broadway stage was the goal of many in the entertainment world. Irving Berlin's songs made their Broadway debut in 1909 and over the next decade they were essential ingredients in the success of many shows. Musical comedies in the first quarter of the twentieth century were often cobbled-together affairs with songs by other writers sprinkled into the score. Called "interpolations," these tunes were written for performers who would literally step out of character and face the audience to sing songs that were unconnected with the show. For Berlin, these performances were similar to vaudeville, and Berlin often wrote for the same performers.

However, as much as he enjoyed and profited from having his songs featured in others' shows, when he wrote his first score in 1914, he demanded that the show include only his songs, a first on Broadway. His initial Broadway scores continued his musical evolution, utilizing a more sophisticated language in both his music and lyrics, and produced enduring standards.

Actor Joseph Santley and the girls he loves appear to have stepped off a *Vogue* magazine cover in *Stop! Look! Listen! Vogue* cover artist Robert McQuinn designed the set and costumes for the show, and one of his illustrations can be seen at left in this photograph.

BROADWAY
1914–1916

For more than a year, Berlin worked on the more than twenty songs in *Watch Your Step*, his first complete Broadway score. He felt it was "the first time Tin Pan Alley got into the legitimate theater." It was at this time that Berlin opened his first music-publishing office to handle his songs for this show and those that followed.

1914

December 8 *Watch Your Step* opens at the New Amsterdam Theatre. A "syncopated musical," the show was a departure from the European operetta tradition and helped chart a new course for the American musical theater.

1915

May 8 *Watch Your Step*, starring Ethel Levey, opens in London.

For his sophomore effort, Berlin had only three months to create another twenty-song score for *Stop! Look! Listen!* Critic Gilbert Seldes wrote in his 1925 book, *The Seven Lively Arts*, "Whatever was gay, light, colorful, whatever was accurate, assured, confident, and good-humored, was in this miraculous production. I saw it twelve times in two weeks."

1915

1916

December 25 *Stop! Look! Listen!* opens at Charles Dillingham's Globe Theatre. One critic wrote that it "was actually the one-man show of Irving Berlin. For once a complete and varied show expressed the spirit of one man to perfection."

February 9 *Follow the Crowd*, the English version of *Stop! Look! Listen!* opens in London.

THE THEATRE

TITLE REG. U. S. PAT. OFF.

35 Cents
$3.50 a Year

MARCH, 1915
VOL. XXI NO. 169

THE MAGAZINE
FOR PLAYGOERS

EV'RYBODY HAS A SYNCOPATED WALK

*"The first great contributor of jazz was an unforgettable revue called
Watch Your Step . . . the hero of this was Irving Berlin, who provided
it with such delicious ragtime songs that the American musical theater
and jazz were thenceforth wedded forever."*

Leonard Bernstein, 1955

Charles Dillingham, derby perpetually cocked over one eye, was second only to Florenz Ziegfeld Jr. in his extravagance. Originally a drama critic for the *New York Sun,* Dillingham decided he could produce better shows than he saw on stage, and made the transition first to manager for Charles Frohman before setting up his own shop. Over thirty years, he produced more than two hundred comedies, plays, musical comedies, and operettas for the Broadway stage. His passion, though, was for vaudeville, and like most producers of the period, he often constructed his shows around the disparate talents of vaudeville performers such as Nora Bayes, Elsie Janis, Walter Kelly, Dave Montgomery, and Fred Stone (whom he had managed since 1906). In the fall of 1914, he had the new season's biggest success in *Chin Chin,* a musical modern-dress version of the Aladdin tale, which relied almost completely on Stone's antics for its popularity. Six weeks later Dillingham would attempt something new for a musical comedy (although not operettas): music and lyrics by a single composer—Irving Berlin. Berlin had insisted that there would be no interpolations and Dillingham agreed, because he understood that a "ragtime" score would be a wonderful attraction on the legitimate stage. After working as a songwriter for only seven years, Berlin was at the top of his profession. He had already written many of the best-selling songs of the period; he was a partner in a publishing firm; and performers were clamoring for his songs.

Although he was called "the Ragtime King,"

With her bobbed hair and slim figure, Irene Castle created a new look for American women.

Vernon and Irene Castle embodied elegant dancing to audiences in the first quarter of the twentieth century.

ABOVE: The Castles at home during the run of *Watch Your Step*. She is wearing a gown designed by Lucille for the spring edition of the show.

BELOW: The principal cast of *Watch Your Step*. (From left to right: the Castles, Frank Tinney, Elizabeth Brice, Charles King, Sallie Fisher, Harry Kelly, and Elizabeth Murray.)

he no longer found the position satisfying. "The thrill of being a successful composer of popular melodies has all gone; that's flat," declared Berlin. "I get no more joy out of knowing that a song of mine has been sold to some two or three million piano players. A million more or less makes no difference now."

He began to talk of writing an opera in ragtime. Like his mentor and idol George M. Cohan, Berlin wanted to Americanize the European idea of the musical, and felt that ragtime was the missing ingredient. "Syncopation is in the soul of every true American, and ragtime is a necessary element of American life. . . . I believe the great American opera of the future will be deliberately based, not on European standards as now, but on typically American standards. A grand opera in syncopation may sound like a joke now—but some day it's going to be a fact—even if I have to write one!" Working for Dillingham was not opera, but it was a step up from both vaudeville and Broadway interpolations.

The Broadway audience would be different too. Berlin's early stage songs were for vaudeville's frequently boisterous audience. Berlin felt comfortable with this mob, and he considered their quick acceptance or rejection of a number a definitive review of his work. A Broadway audience was more refined, more genteel, and more educated. Berlin understood that now he would be writing for the show's characters rather than for individual performers. As he began to work on the score

A NOTABLE GROUP IN "WATCH YOUR STEP" AT THE NEW AMSTERDAM THEATRE

IRVING BERLIN'S SHOW BUSINESS

in the summer of 1913, even his interpolated numbers for other productions evolved from solo star turns into duets between the characters of the musical he was contributing to.

Dillingham titled this show *Watch Your Step* after he hired dancers Vernon and Irene Castle as its featured performers. The Castles had come to epitomize ballroom dancing to American audiences by taking the socially unacceptable "dancing craze" (fueled by Berlin tunes) and making it seem elegant and unthreatening. They soon were ubiquitous, appearing in cabarets, dance schools, and vaudeville, although Irene Castle would later say, "Our best work on the stage was done in *Watch Your Step.*" Dillingham, in his typical fashion, soon made the show a revue of top-drawer vaudeville entertainment, with comedian Frank Tinney, Tempest and Sunshine (a dancing-sisters act), Doyle and Dixon ("the classiest two-man hoofing act in show biz"), and Harry Kelly's dog act. The show had so much talent that after its first Syracuse tryout, Dillingham fired W. C. Fields, whose bit was the hit of the show, because it slowed the first act and his top-billed stars were unhappy that he stole their limelight. Charles King, Sallie Fisher, and Elizabeth Brice were the performers who carried most of the singing chores.

Debuting just as World War I started, *Watch Your Step*'s program proudly proclaimed that it was "Made in America." American music and dancing were ultramodern, and Berlin was at the forefront. One review asked, "Why import music made in Vienna when you can get it from Berlin?" The combination of syncopation, vaudeville, contemporary design, and a wisecracking attitude could only be found in America. Two years later, Picasso, Jean Cocteau, and Erik Satie would take these same elements to create their legendary ballet, *Parade.* Both productions, though clearly different in intent, identified movement as the spark that made the entertainment so vibrant.

Dillingham's *Chin Chin* revolved around the song and dance act of Dave Montgomery and Fred Stone. Another loose revue of vaudeville performers in a lavish setting, it was at the mercy of its performers. The strength of *Watch Your Step* was its music. Although Dillingham larded the program with dancing acts and dog acts, when the production went on tour, audiences did not miss the Castles or any of the original principals. The score was clearly the star.

Songs from the score were the first to be published by Irving Berlin Music, Inc. In December 1914, Berlin decided that he would

ABOVE: In *Watch Your Step* Elizabeth Brice introduced "Move Over," set in a Pullman train car. She also sang duets with her regular partner Charles King, even recording one, "I've Gotta Go Back to Texas."

ABOVE LEFT AND BELOW: Thelma Cudlipp's sketches of Frank Tinney, a languid blackface vaudeville comedian once described as having "the quality of a mischievous kid when he was telling a joke," and Vernon Castle, who also played drums in the show.

Verdi - To change my song would be unlawful
Cho - not to change it would be awful
Verdi - Stop
Cho - we're goin' a rag it
Verdi - Stop
Cho - we're goin' a rag it
Verdi - Stop
Cho - we're goin' a rag it
Verdi - Stop
Cho - we're goin' a rag it
Verdi - No
Cho - rag - rag - rag rag your Rigolettos
Verdi - I - No

ABOVE: The centerpiece of the second act of *Watch Your Step* was an extended opera parody in which Berlin quoted and "ragged" Verdi's work until, as these handwritten lyrics show, the composer's ghost appears and begs for it to stop.

RIGHT: The chorus of *Watch Your Step* fancifully dressed by Helen Dryden.

OPPOSITE: Gaby Deslys and Joseph Santley in *Stop! Look! Listen!* Gaby's headgear was evidently much more memorable than her talents. Santley would work again with Berlin in the *Music Box Revues*.

publish his "theater" songs separately from Waterson and Snyder. By 1917 he decided to publish all of his music on his own. His firm's motto would soon be "Standards of the World: 'Sterling' on Silver, 'Irving Berlin' on Songs." *Watch Your Step* only generated one hit in "Simple Melody," his first signature counterpoint song, which set a nostalgic tune against a syncopated one, interlacing the words and the melodies of both songs into a gorgeous mix. The show's success kept Berlin's name in front of the public for many months. Berlin understood the value of the emerging power of the media and carefully stoked it to get the exposure he wanted. From the time of "Alexander's Ragtime Band," his success story was common knowledge. Outside of show business, many of his friends were writers and journalists, who also made a living from observing the world around them.

Watch Your Step was a hit. At its one-hundredth performance, Berlin appeared on stage with the Castles and sang from his songbook to the crowd's delight. Six months later, the show was a success in London. But as one newspaper wag put it, "Nothing could say more for Irving Berlin's production music than Mr. Dillingham did when he produced a second "Berlin show." In September 1915, the songwriter began work on a show that eventually was titled as *Stop! Look! Listen!*

To give *Watch Your Step* a modern look to go with its fresh syncopated score, producer Charles Dillingham engaged two signature *Vogue* artists of the period to design its sets, costumes, and print publicity. Dillingham was as well versed in fashion and proper society as he was in the two-a-day performers of vaudeville. Both *Watch Your Step* and *Stop! Look! Listen!* were to have what one newspaperman said was "that air of smartness of *tout ce qu'il y a de plus chic* that characterizes everything sponsored by Mr. Dillingham."

According to Helen Dryden, Dillingham had seen a powder puff that she had sketched in the pages of *Vogue,* and he asked her to create costumes for the show. Undoubtedly, he had seen many of the sophisticated, decorative *Vogue* covers she had designed since 1910. The clean lines and colorful palette of her fashion drawing were inspired by Leon Bakst's

designs for the Ballets Russes and Paul Poiret's French fashion plates. *Watch Your Step* was her first attempt at costume design and she was delighted. She said after the opening that "to experiment for once with beautiful materials instead of paints, and to see the creations of my brush living and dancing, is a joy for thousands of beauty-loving eyes." Dryden used for the costumes the same bold, flat colors that she had used in her illustration work. Like many of her cover creations, the costumes were trimmed in fur.

Vogue artists were ideal for audiences who looked to Broadway, the upscale form of popular entertainment, for its fashion trends. Fashion was so important for performers that Sallie Fisher, who was featured in *Watch Your Step,* remarked, "Inability to wear clothes well keeps girls out of the chorus as well as out of principal parts. I have heard

managers say, 'Yes, Wilson is a good-looking girl, but we can't use her in the chorus... she can't wear clothes.' In these days of the gorgeously gowned chorus, that means a lot."

Berlin understood the importance of fashion. *Stop! Look! Listen!* opens in the costume shop of a theater with the chorus girls singing:

That the shows that are successes
Are made so by the dresses
That are worn by the chorus girls.
They must be of the latest fashion,
And each a perfect fit;
They help to bring the cash in
And make the show a hit.

Watch Your Step was inevitably described as "a riot of color." The show opened in a "Law Office de Danse" which presented stenographers in blue velvet trimmed in white. "Then came girls in tan taffeta frocks, the skirts very full and edged in coral velvet. A few wore gray and coral." Robert McQuinn, another *Vogue* artist who set the look of magazine covers, gave the sets a stylish patina. When the curtain rose, the first scene had a "modern, almost a cubist" design, according to one review. Another concluded, "The entire production had an air of up-to-datedness."

McQuinn took over all design duties for *Stop! Look! Listen!*, and some reviewers felt that the show's success owed a great deal to his work. "[T]here is nothing in the book and score to compete seriously with the costumes and scenery of Robert McQuinn," wrote Heywood Broun in his opening-night review. "A set in the second act, 'At the Farm,' is the most beautiful stage picture we have ever seen. Done in flat splotches of lilac and one dot of red, this picture fondled the eye as Gaby in all her glory never caressed it." Using much of the same color palette that he employed in his cover work, McQuinn was also singled out for his Hawaiian beach scene "of gorgeous yellow sands edging a deep blue sea." He primarily used painted flats and drops to create bold, impressionistic stage pictures that proved to be an effective backdrop for Berlin's songs.

OPPOSITE: Robert McQuinn's set for the opening scene in *Watch Your Step*, "A Law Office de Danse."

LEFT: A Helen Dryden cover for *Vogue*. Dryden brought her covers to life with her costumes for *Watch Your Step*.

ABOVE: Helen Dryden's homage to both designer Poiret and the commedia dell'arte character Pierrot.

ABOVE, LEFT: Gaby Deslys's various head-gear of "Woolworthian height" did not disappoint. As one critic wrote, "Once again everything goes to Gaby's head."

ABOVE, RIGHT: Joseph Santley with his fall, winter, summer, and spring loves, who have stepped off the cover of *Vogue* in "The Girl on the Magazine." (From left to right: Evelyn Conway, Hazel Lewis, Marion Davies, Eleanor St. Clair). William Randolph Hearst first fell in love with Davies when he saw her in this show.

Dillingham assembled much of the group he had for the first show, with Harry Smith again writing the "book" and some of the same acts engaged for the production. He hired French actress and former mistress of the king of Portugal, Gaby Deslys, as the show's star. Gaby, as she was known to all, could neither sing nor dance very well. Her English was barely understandable, but as one review declared, audiences were not required to hear the show's simple story of "only a chorus girl now, but just you wait." Heywood Broun wrote, "We waited, but finally a man came around and locked up the theatre. Gaby is passably pretty, but distinctly a minor artist. One cannot watch her overlong without impatience." Audiences, however, were interested in what outlandish hats or costumes she might wear. According to the costume list, Gaby wore nine gowns in the first act alone.

Berlin had quickly adapted to the specifications of the stage, but he was also servicing his growing publishing business. *Stop! Look! Listen!* yielded two standards: "I Love a Piano" and "The Girl on the Magazine." "I Love a Piano" was introduced in the first act by Harry Fox against an unbroken line of black-and-white keyboards that stretched the width of the stage. While six pianists were "forging ragtime" on the pianos, there were chorus girls dancing on a mezzanine above and down a double staircase. Berlin's paean to his instrument was not a well integrated number, but it was a wonderful set piece. "The Girl on the Magazine" was at least partly inspired by designer Robert McQuinn's work for *Vogue;* in fact, the girls that male lead Joseph Santley sang about stepped right off covers of *Vogue.* Billy Murray's recording of the former and Harry MacDonough's recording of the latter made up the first double-sided number-one hit record ever in May 1916.

The show's success was immediate, but unfortunately for all involved, not long-lived. Gaby and her husband/manager Harry Pilcer, who was also in the show, soon soured on each other, and Gaby's performances became lackluster. Unlike Berlin's first show, *Stop! Look! Listen!* relied heavily on its star attractions, and when word got out that Gaby was no longer worth seeing, the show closed after only three months.

Nevertheless, the two shows confirmed Berlin's transition from a Tin Pan Alley songwriter to composer. Historian Charles Hamm concluded that with these productions Berlin had "mastered the techniques of writing for the legitimate theater as opposed to the vaudeville house or the home circle." He had succeeded in song publishing, and had already had considerable success on records. If he had not composed the opera of his dream, he certainly seemed capable of it, yet the opera would have to wait. Berlin soon received word that he was needed for a much more important job.

ABOVE: Harry Fox, who introduced the classic "I Love a Piano."

BELOW: The finale of *Stop! Look! Listen!* featured a Berlin counterpoint song ragging the syncopated "When I Get Back to the U.S.A." against "My Country 'tis of Thee." For the West End production, Berlin revised the lyric to get back to "London Town" and set it against "God Save the Queen."

Like most Tin Pan Alley tunesmiths, Irving Berlin knew that current events were a good source of material for songs. As Europe went to war in 1914, he wrote the ironic, antiwar "Stay Down Here Where You Belong," in which the Devil counsels his son not to go "up there, my son/I know you'd be surprised/You'll find a lot people who are not civilized." He would later be embarrassed by the song's sentiment and its quality. In 1917 Berlin wrote an "official recruiting song," "For Your Country and My Country." He never made it clear who asked for it and who had made it "official."

When Berlin himself was drafted toward the end of World War I, he worked as hard at being a good soldier as he did at everything else. His late-night working habits as a songwriter, however, soon collided with the early rising of a soldier. Berlin sized up the situation and did what he did best: he wrote a song about it. "Oh! How I Hate to Get Up in the Morning," was the start of a journey that began at Camp Upton in Long Island and ended at the Lexington Theatre on Broadway in a morale-boosting, fund-raising revue about soldiers that Berlin wrote and staged, titled *Yip, Yip, Yaphank*.

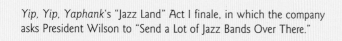

Yip, Yip, Yaphank's "Jazz Land" Act I finale, in which the company asks President Wilson to "Send a Lot of Jazz Bands Over There."

AMERICA
1914–1918

Patriotic Songs in a Syncopated Style

1914

1915

1917

"They're on Their Way to Mexico"
Berlin's first patriotic song celebrated the troops sent to deal with, in Berlin's words, "the trouble with Mexico."

"Stay Down Here Where You Belong"
Apparently written for *Watch Your Step*, this ironic "war" song later became a favorite of Groucho Marx, who sang it on many occasions in the 1950s.

"While the Band Played an American Rag"
A fantasy song in which world leaders stop "war talk" and drink to each other while "a German band/played an American, made-in-America,/an American rag."

"Let's All Be Americans Now"
With war declared, Berlin implored listeners to do their duty and fight for their country.

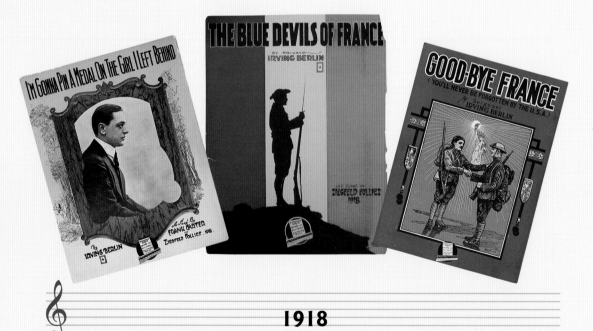

Berlin writes more than ten songs during World War I that cover the spectrum of genres and emotions. Typically for Berlin, almost all of the songs center on soldiers' lives and experiences and reveal the human heart of international conflict.

1918

"I'm Gonna Pin a Medal on the Girl I Left Behind"
Introduced in the *Ziegfeld Follies of 1918* by Frank Carter, who sings about the bravery of his girl who stays strong while he is off fighting.

"The Blue Devils of France"
Another 1918 *Follies* hit, this one introduced by Lillian Lorraine and ensemble, celebrating the courageous French military unit famous for blue uniforms with flowing cape and beret.

"Good-bye France"
Published at the end of the war, Berlin paid homage to French soldiers who, he declared, would "never be forgotten by the U.S.A."

1917 1918

"For Your Country and My Country"
This recruiting song instructed listeners: "We know you love your USA/but if you want the world to know it,/now's the time to show it;/your uncle Sammy needs you one and all—/answer to his call."

"They Were All Out of Step But Jim"
This comic song featured parents whose pride in seeing their son Jim in a parade makes them blind to the fact that he is out of step with his company.

"The Devil Has Brought Up All the Coal"
Berlin finds a way to boost morale during a coal shortage by telling listeners that the devil is hoarding the fuel to see that "There'll be a hot time in Hades/when the Kaiser gets there."

"Over the Sea Boys"
Berlin's navy song describes that while the sailors have left "wives behind/for fighting of a diff'rent kind" their thoughts are "with the land we love ever in mind."

Berlin "ragged" the army long before he was drafted. Here is an illustrated song slide from Berlin's 1912 hit "Ragtime Soldier Man."

EVER SINCE I
PUT ON A UNIFORM

*"I sweat blood between three and six [on] many mornings, and when the
drops that fall off my forehead hit the paper, they're notes."*
Irving Berlin describing his songwriting routine

For Berlin, the most fertile time to write was at
night, long after others had gone to sleep. In his
apartment on West Seventieth Street he wrapped his piano hammers with cotton
to muffle the sounds so as not to wake his neighbors, but the desire—the need—to
write another hit tune is what kept him up. He often had his musical secretary on
hand to take down the melody he dreamed up. If the secretary went home, he
knew he could expect to be awakened, no matter what hour, by a call from Berlin to
transcribe a piece of music played over the phone. Berlin's Sisyphean task was to
satisfy the public's insatiable desire for new songs, and he estimated he wrote nine
bad songs for every one that he thought good enough to keep. Fortunately for
Berlin, his successes made him enough money to bankroll a nice apartment, with
an office, a staff, and a chauffeur, to take care of all his needs.

Ragtime had become Jazz, and Berlin was considered by people around the
world as the progenitor of American music. He recognized that only in America was
there the opportunity to succeed as he had done. These were probably among the
factors in his decision to become a citizen of the United States. On February 26,
1918, a little more than a year after he published "Let's All Be Americans Now," he
was naturalized as one. Three months later he was drafted. The induction notice
came as a surprise to the songwriter, as he had frequently made the rounds of doctors and specialists in New York to help him with his indigestion and insomnia,
and had often been told that the army would
never take him. When he heard the news, and
aware of how unsuited Berlin would be to military
life, the writer and con man Wilson Mizner joked

The cover of the *Yip, Yip, Yaphank*
souvenir program.

"U.S. Takes Berlin" was the
apocryphal headline when the
songwriter was drafted in 1918.

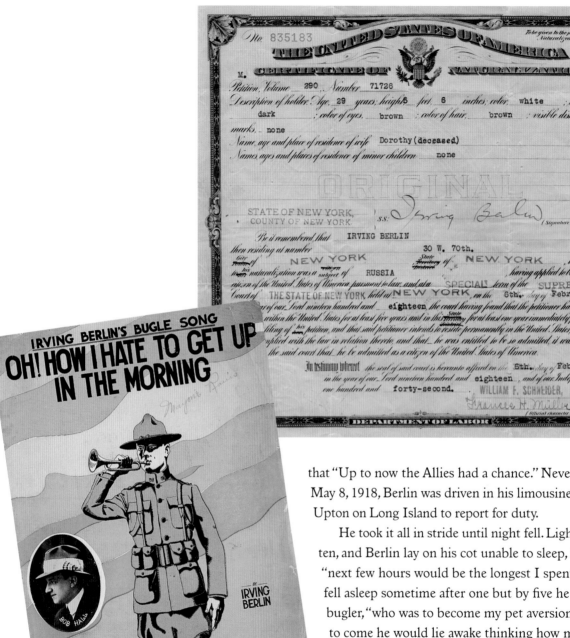

that "Up to now the Allies had a chance." Nevertheless, on May 8, 1918, Berlin was driven in his limousine to Camp Upton on Long Island to report for duty.

He took it all in stride until night fell. Lights-out was at ten, and Berlin lay on his cot unable to sleep, feeling that the "next few hours would be the longest I spent in my life." He fell asleep sometime after one but by five he heard the bugler, "who was to become my pet aversion." In the nights to come he would lie awake thinking how much he hated reveille. "But I wanted to be a good soldier," recalled Berlin a half-century later, "so every morning when the bugle blew I'd jump right out of bed just as if I liked getting up early. The other soldiers thought I was a little too eager about it and they hated me. That's why I finally wrote a song about it."

"Oh! How I Hate to Get Up in the Morning," was classic Berlin. The title summed up the song's sentiment, and the sentiment tapped the vernacular of American life. While he wrote specifically about the soldier's life, civilians at every stratum of society could relate to it. Its infectious tune even appropriates the sound of reveille to the words:

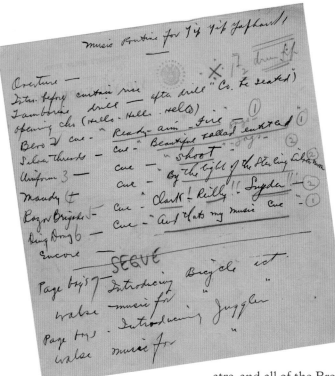

You've got to get up,
You've got to get up,
You've got to get up this morning.

When the navy staged a musical fundraiser titled *Biff! Bang!*, Private Berlin's commanding officer called him in to help put together a show that would raise money for a service club at Camp Upton where soldiers could meet their families. Berlin agreed, but pointed out that he did his best work at night. He was excused from reveille and soon worked in his own barracks to write the show and its songs. Eventually the production, titled *Yip, Yip, Yaphank*, would feature 300 servicemen, including actors, directors, and dancers transferred from other companies to be in the show. Plans were made for two weeks of performances in August 1918 at the cavernous Century Theatre, and all of the Broadway *haut monde* dutifully trooped up to West Sixty-second Street to do their patriotic bit. No one had any hope that the production would be anything other than a modest morale-booster and fund-raiser. Yet according to one report, "the coldest audience in the world became a carefree mob that whistled,

shouted, and cheered every number, and joined in the choruses after the first encore."

Berlin, a first-time producer, had put together a revue that mixed army inside jokes, a minstrel show, female impersonators, and patriotism into an exhilarating night of theater. His songs were stories from Camp Upton, whether it was the bore of drinking nonalcoholic beer, or K.P., to accompany both staged numbers and army drills. Of the 300 members of the company, only twenty had appeared on stage before, yet Berlin, with the help of director Private Will H. Smith, had whipped them into a state of precision that Ziegfeld would have been proud of. As *Variety* stated, "It's only show people who may fully appreciate what that means." After the show on opening night, Berlin treated the whole company to ham, eggs, and coffee at Child's restaurant.

The show ran two weeks at the Century, but with the Broadway season just starting, it was forced to leave to make way for a prearranged new tenant; it then played another two weeks at the Lexington Theatre.

OPPOSITE, TOP: Berlin's handwritten production notes show how involved he was in every aspect of *Yip, Yip, Yaphank*.

OPPOSITE, BELOW: Besides the army humor, many of the laughs in the show came from the sight of manly recruits dressed as chorus girls.

LEFT: Ninety soldiers to a barracks at Camp Upton was a far cry from Berlin's comfortable bachelor pad on West Seventieth Street.

           IRVING BERLIN'S SHOW BUSINESS

Every day the company practiced their drills for two hours in Central Park and acted as a normal army troop. Instead of facing a hostile enemy on the Western Front, they faced cheering audiences on Central Park West. While Berlin's mentor, George M. Cohan, had written the signature song of the war, "Over There," Berlin was just as clearly identified as an American patriot. And in capturing the spirit of what Americans felt when

> Against my wishes
> I wash the dishes,
> To make the wide world
> Safe for democracy,

audiences felt he was one of them. He understood the work, as well as the glory, in serving his country.

Despite the fact that *Yip, Yip, Yaphank* raised more than twice the amount needed to build the service club, the structure was never erected. With the war coming to a close, the base was soon unnecessary. But for Berlin, a new chapter was opening in his life.

OPPOSITE: "Poor little he/He's a KP," sang the chorus, "He scrubs the mess hall/Upon bended knee. But when he begins to fraternize with these 'lovelies from the *Follies*,' the sergeant yells 'Berlin? Back to the kitchen.'"

ABOVE: Berlin introduced "The Sterling Silver Moon" as a minstrel number in *Yip, Yip, Yaphank* and one year later would adapt it for one of the great hits of the *Ziegfeld Follies*: "Mandy."

The mélange of acts in vaudeville set the stage for the Broadway revue, a combination of songs, skits, dance, and satire. Although Ziegfeld claimed he introduced the form in his first *Follies* in 1907, revues in America go back to the Civil War. By the twenties they were a staple on Broadway and a showcase for Tin Pan Alley. Over the next decade Berlin wrote for little else on Broadway. From a creative standpoint—judging by the array of wonderful songs he wrote for revues—he enjoyed the freedom to choose his subjects and style. From a business standpoint, a production number provided a visual presentation that would make a song all the more memorable, much as a music video does today. Although he would later have success with "situations shows," as he called book musicals on Broadway, in his films he often used a revue as the performance context of his songs.

The top presenters of his day, including Ziegfeld, Dillingham, Frohman, and the Shuberts, all worked with Berlin. When Sam Harris offered him the chance to build his own theater to house his revues, Berlin helped to redefine the genre, elevating its star attraction from sex to song. For four seasons, Berlin and his creative team initiated a more intimate revue that gathered the best singers, comedians, and designers to manufacture an effervescent show that beguiled audiences and critics.

Joseph Urban designed this "celestial staircase" for *The Century Girl* in 1916. Staircases became a signature element of all succeeding *Ziegfeld Follies*.

BIRTH·OF·CENTVRY·GIRL

BROADWAY
1916–1927

A Review of Revues: A Chronology of Berlin Contributions

1916

1918

Ziegfeld Follies of 1916
New Amsterdam Theatre, opened June 12, 1916. 112 performances. "In Florida among the Palms" is featured.

The Century Girl
Century Theatre, opened November 6, 1916. 200 performances. A score split between Victor Herbert and Berlin, featuring Berlin's "The Chicken Walk" and "Alice in Wonderland."

The Cohan Revue of 1918
New Amsterdam Theatre, opened December 31, 1917. 96 performances. Cohan invites Berlin to be the only other songwriter for his satirical revue, and Berlin's songs steal the show.

Ziegfeld Follies of 1918
New Amsterdam Theatre, opened June 18, 1918. 151 performances. Still working on the score of *Yip, Yip, Yaphank*, Berlin continues the patriotic mood with "I'm Going to Pin a Medal on the Girl I Left Behind" and "The Blue Devils of France."

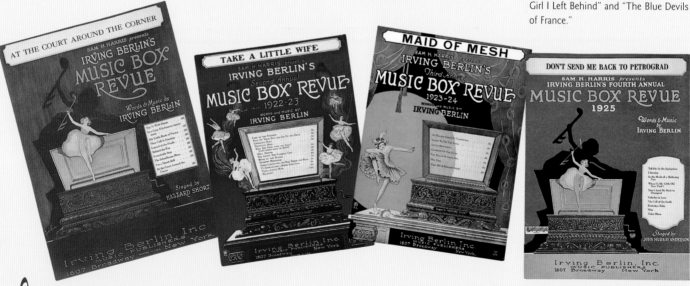

1921

1922

1923

1924

The Music Box Revue (1921–22)
Music Box Theatre, opened September 22, 1921. 440 performances. Features the Music Box theme song, "Say It with Music," in addition to "Everybody Step."

The Music Box Revue (1922–23)
Music Box Theatre, opened October 23, 1922. 330 performances. Of Berlin's ten songs, "Lady of the Evening" and "Pack Up Your Sins and Go to the Devil" are among the revue's highlights.

The Music Box Revue (1923–24)
Music Box Theatre, opened September 22, 1923. 273 performances. Later "What'll I Do?" is interpolated into the ten-song score.

The Music Box Revue (1924–25)
Music Box Theatre, opened December 1, 1924. 184 performances. Grace Moore singing "Tell Her in the Springtime" and Fanny Brice pleading "Don't Send Me Back to Petrograd" are among the nearly twenty songs of the show.

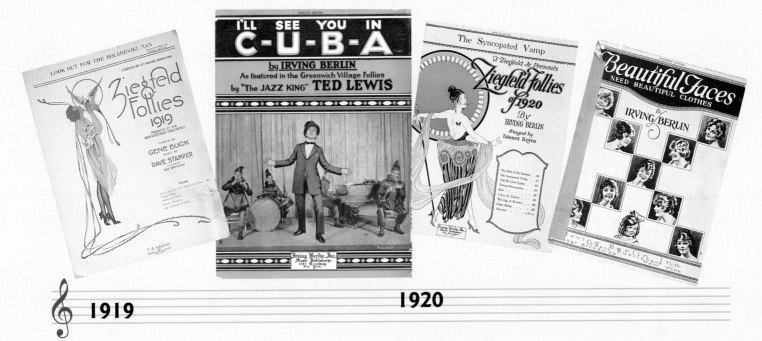

1919 · 1920

Ziegfeld Follies of 1919
New Amsterdam Theatre, opened June 16, 1919. 171 performances. The first act is exclusively Berlin songs, including "A Pretty Girl Is like a Melody." Eddie Cantor later introduces the suggestive "You'd Be Surprised" during its New York run.

The Greenwich Village Follies
Greenwich Village Theatre, opened July 15, 1919. 232 performances. Berlin writes about escaping the confines of Prohibition with a knowing wink in "I'll See You in C-U-B-A."

Ziegfeld Follies of 1920
New Amsterdam Theatre, opened June 22, 1920. 123 performances. Production features seven Berlin songs, including "The Girl of My Dreams" and "Tell Me, Little Gypsy."

Broadway Brevities of 1920
Winter Garden Theatre, opened September 29, 1920. 105 performances. Edith Hallor and "the girls" introduce "Beautiful Faces Need Beautiful Clothes," a number dropped from the *Follies of 1919*.

1927

Ziegfeld Follies of 1927
New Amsterdam Theatre, opened August 16, 1927. 167 performances. The first *Follies* to have a score by only one composer.

Berlin (at piano) with Eddie Cantor, Ziegfeld (center), and dance director Sammy Lee (right) at a rehearsal of the *Ziegfeld Follies of 1927*.

SO SAY IT WITH A BEAUTIFUL SONG

"I have to have another song! Look at these costumes." So declared Florenz Ziegfeld, after Berlin had finished his part of the score for the *Follies of 1919.* Ziegfeld showed Berlin five costume sketches and said, "I have to have a number for them." Berlin had already written ten songs for the show, but took the sketches home nevertheless. With tenor John Steel making his debut in the *Follies,* Berlin had the idea of writing a lyric to five different classical melodies to go with each girl and gown. "But I had to have a song to introduce the number and close it. Then I wrote the lyrics and music to fit the action." This was the Ziegfeld Girl number where showgirls dressed in opulent costumes descended a long staircase. It appeared in every *Follies,* and Berlin wrote what would become the anthem of the series, "A Pretty Girl Is like a Melody." Berlin later said, "It wasn't the hit of the show—'Tulip Time' was the hit then—'Pretty Girl' has become the hit." He had once again left his signature on another part of American popular culture.

Ziegfeld's shows were the best showcase any songwriter could hope for. Ziegfeld had been producing since the turn of the century; his *Follies,* started in 1907, had become the rage of New York. The producer's recipe of mixing popular American entertainment and European high-culture sensibilities had redefined the revue in America, making it seem more clever, more tuneful, and most of all more exciting, than just about any other show on the Great White Way.

The Ziegfeld motto was "Glorifying the American Girl," and he had learned early in his career that a little skin went a long way in heightening interest in his productions. Although the nudity of his shows is more legend than fact (perpetuated by his photographer Alfred Cheney Johnson's penchant for pictures of the *Follies* girls wearing very little), the *frisson* of sex, song, and settings he invented was a potent force on Broadway for more than twenty years.

In 1916, Ziegfeld and Charles Dillingham joined forces to operate the cavernous Century

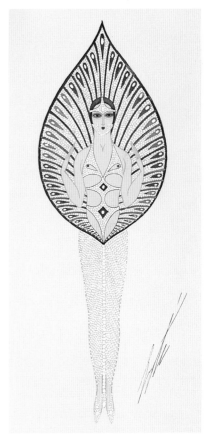

Berlin brought fashion designer and illustrator Erté to America to design this costume and others for the *Music Box Revues.*

Members of the chorus from the *Ziegfeld Follies of 1927* represent virtually the full range of costumes seen in the annual revue.

Theatre north of the theater district. Both had worked recently with Berlin. Dillingham had opened *Stop! Look! Listen!* less than a year earlier, and the *Ziegfeld Follies of 1916* had provided another hit for Berlin, "In Florida among the Palms." The producers asked Berlin to share the composing duties for their inaugural production, dubbed simply *The Century Girl*, with Victor Herbert, the dean of American popular song. Berlin accepted but was concerned with how his work might compare to the classically trained Herbert's. Over lunch, Berlin asked Herbert if he should formally study music, and the composer of many classics, including *Babes in Toyland,* assured him that he might lose the simplicity that made his work unique. Berlin eventually did try taking music lessons, but after two days he quit, feeling that in the time he spent practicing he could have written more songs.

Despite Herbert and Berlin's best efforts, their work was overshadowed by Joseph Urban's sets, especially the introduction of one of Ziegfeld's most iconic elements, the "celestial" staircase on which beauties strolled down in extravagant costumes, and Dillingham's vaudeville smorgasbord, which included Marie Dressler, Frank Tinney, Elsie Janis, Doyle and Dixon, and Sam Bernhard. The opening night was more than four hours long, yet the show became a hit, running for more than 200 performances.

LEON ERROL AND ELSIE JANIS
In "The Century Girl"

Leon Errol staged "The Chicken Walk," although he did not perform in it. Here he is shown in costume with Elsie Janis as "The Chicken" in the first-act finale of *The Century Girl*, "Hunting for a New Dance."

Both impresarios admired Berlin, and later donated costumes and sets to *Yip, Yip, Yaphank,* which was presented at their Century Theatre. Berlin continued to contribute to both producers' efforts, writing two World War I numbers for the *Follies of 1918,* which opened two months before his army show, and to Dillingham's *Everything,* which opened three days later. When George M. Cohan asked Berlin to share the songwriting duties with him for his *Cohan Revue of 1918,* a satirical show lampooning current Broadway hits, Cohan found himself playing second fiddle in the reviews. One remarked, "The generosity of Cohan in inviting contributions from Irving Berlin is proved by the fact that the Berlin numbers are in most cases superior to Cohan's." Nevertheless, the following year Berlin wrote "That Revolutionary Rag" as an interpolation for Cohan's operetta *The Royal Vagabond.*

The revue that Ziegfeld had popularized in America was more Berlin's milieu than the Cohan operettas or Dillingham productions. The *Follies of 1919,* considered by many to be the apotheosis of the series because of its stars, sets, girls, and songs, featured nine Berlin numbers when it opened. "Sterling Moon" from *Yip, Yip, Yaphank* was revised and called "Mandy." It was part of the minstrel show first-act finale, with Eddie Cantor, Bert Williams, and George Lemaire as blackface minstrels. The singing duo of Van and Schenck came on crooning the song with John Steele and Eddie Dowling. Marilyn Miller, dressed in pink satin, did a soft-shoe number as the chorus around her tapped. Ray Dooley as Mandy had ten other blackfaced chorus girls in tow, all dressed like Miller. Nearly fifty years later Berlin

A Model-Show Girl and Mr. Frank Carter's Bride

Toon Heanley July 20th 1919

"MAURESETTE" AND MARILYN MILLER IN THE "ZIEGFELD FOLLIES"

"Mauresette" is a Lucile model and, in common with all Lucile models, hides her identity behind a fanciful name. She is *Oil* in "The Follies Salad," an orientally degagée lady in the "Harem Number," and *Humoresque* in "A Pretty Girl is Like a Melody." After the music she takes to drink—soft drink—and becomes *Bevo* in "A Saloon of the Future." Marilyn Miller, (Mrs. Frank Carter) at the right, is effervescent as *George Primrose* in the Minstrel number, in which she clogs daintily before Eddie Cantor, Bert Williams and George Lemaire as *Tambo, Bones* and *Middleman* would remember that "Everyone still thinks that [the *Follies of 1919*] was the best *Follies* Ziegfeld ever had and the Minstrel Finale was the high spot."

The year 1919 also saw the first serious competition to Ziegfeld with the debut of other revues such as *George White's Scandals* and *The Greenwich Village Follies.* Soon the competition would also include former Ziegfeld dancer Earl Carroll's *Vanities,* Dillingham's *Nifties* and many others. Ziegfeld had helped to popularize the revue on Broadway and now he watched as his primacy in the genre slowly slipped away.

In 1920 Berlin contributed another seven songs to that year's edition of the *Follies,* although none were to become standards. Berlin might have been content to contribute to the *Ziegfeld Follies* and a few other productions had producer Sam Harris not called. A few years earlier at a Friars Club gathering, Berlin had suggested that Harris devote a theater to musical comedy and call it The Music Box. Harris had bought some property on Forty-fifth Street in the theater district and was ready to help Berlin make his idea a reality.

Harris was an ideal associate for Berlin. He too had grown up on the Lower East Side, working odd jobs before managing the boxer "Terrible Terry" McGovern, who became the lightweight champ. Harris got the pugilist into vaudeville, and Harris was soon bitten by the theater bug. Working with his friend George M. Cohan, he first produced Cohan's smash *Little Johnny Jones.* The two had had a successful partnership until the summer of 1919, when the Equity strike caused a rift (with Harris siding with actors over managers) and the two separated amicably. Harris, who had visited the Pelham Café when Berlin was a singing waiter, had met the songwriter professionally in Chicago in 1913 when they were both involved in the show *Are You a Mason?* that died there. By 1920 Harris had a sterling reputation, not only as a successful producer, but also as an honest businessman. Berlin was attracted to his offer, and the two arranged to build their Music Box. It would be the first Broadway theater to feature the work of only one songwriter: Irving Berlin.

Harris and Berlin were chagrined to see that the high quality they demanded for their theater caused the budget to rapidly expand. When Berlin told his old friend Joe Schenck, now a successful film producer, that he had a problem, Schenck asked, "Who is she?" Schenck readily agreed to help by putting up half of Berlin's 50 percent. The group would eventually spend nearly one million

OPPOSITE: Ziegfeld's motto was "Glorifying the American Girl," and he stocked the *Follies* with beautiful women. Some had a talent to look good, while others had talent *and* looked good. He loved Marilyn Miller and made her the star of several shows, although she never reciprocated that love.

ABOVE: After the *Ziegfeld Follies of 1919* opened, Eddie Cantor incorporated Berlin's suggestive "You'd Be Surprised" into the show to great success. The song was such a hit that George Jessel made it part of his act at the Winter Garden and Lew Cooper also sang it in the revue he was starring in. Berlin's publishing house did not hesitate to include all three on the sheet music cover.

dollars to bring the theater to life and another $188,000 to stage the first *Music Box Revue.*

Berlin had learned from Ziegfeld and Dillingham, and with his own new-found flair as a producer, coupled with Harris's extensive experience, he felt ready to be in direct competition. Berlin and Harris took a chance on the untested Hassard Short to stage the production and literally put their money into making their revue funnier, prettier, and more tuneful than any other. Short staged rich spectacles in the intimate setting of the theater, and brought together a talented set of designers to transform his extravagant ideas into fantastic costumes. In their more intimate revue, sexy costumes were not the star attraction. Comedians Sam Bernard and William Collier were responsible for the laughs. Even Berlin appeared in a piece called "An Interview," with eight chorus girls (called the Eight Reporters) questioning the composer in song about his many hits. By the end he was singing his latest, "All by Myself." For this first *Music Box Revue* in 1921, he wrote the theme song for the theater, "Say It with Music." Another song, "Everybody Step," was lauded by the distinguished American composer John Alden

BELOW: The back cover of sheet music from the *Music Box Revue of 1921.*

OPPOSITE: Director Hassard Short presented Berlin with the original artwork for the program cover on the opening night of the Music Box Theatre.

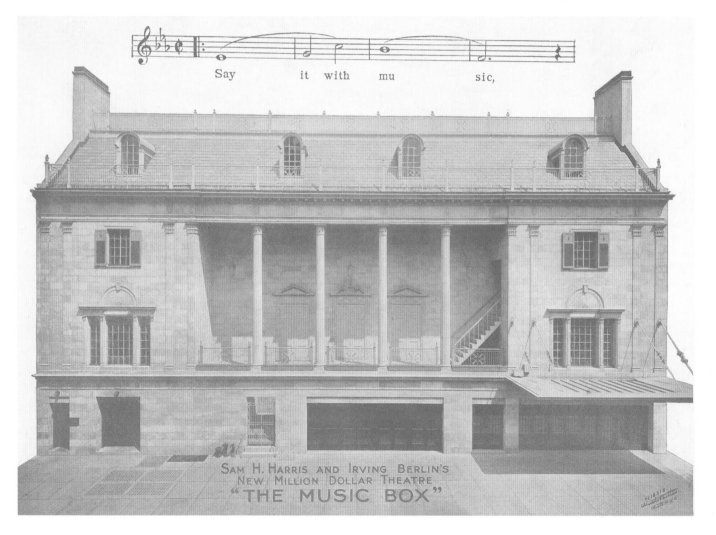

IRVING BERLIN'S SHOW BUSINESS

The 1920s saw the emergence of the "ballyhoo" of Broadway, a convergence of mass media and press agentry that filled newspapers and magazines with fantastic stories of the Great White Way. Berlin and the lavish staging of the *Music Box Revues* supplied great stories and images for the emerging national press.

Photo Abbe

One of the prettiest and most novel features of Irving Berlin's dazzlingly beautiful "Music Box Revue" is a dancing act called "Dining Out." Ivy Sawyer and Joseph Santley, pictured above, are the diners. They arrive at the restaurant where they are welcomed with great ceremony, seat themselves at the table which is then hoisted to the balcony as shown. Then, up from the archway underneath, come the delicacies they are to eat. First the oysters, as seen above, followed by all the other dishes in proper sequence

SCENE IN "THE MUSIC BOX REVUE"

Victor Georg

HELEN RICH

Who takes the part of the little Oriental boy in the Chinese Porcelains number of the Music Box Revue

ABOVE: Berlin and producer and partner Sam Harris. Ethel Waters described Sam Harris as "a true showman, and the money he made on his hits was only something he was glad to get because it meant he would be able to put on more shows."

LEFT: Detail of Sam Harris's stationery.

OPPOSITE: The Brox Sisters (Bobbe, Lorayne, and Patricia) in full regalia. They first appeared on Broadway in the inaugural *Music Box Revue* in 1921 introducing "Everybody Step," the start of a decade-long connection to Berlin. They were in three of the four *Music Box Revues*, plus the all-Berlin 1927 *Ziegfeld Follies*. They recorded a number of Berlin tunes for the Victor and Brunswick labels throughout the 1920s. Toward the end of the decade, they appeared in several Vitaphone shorts and three feature films before retiring in 1930.

Carpenter as one of the "masterpieces of musical art," along with works by Wagner, Beethoven, and Chopin. Berlin was delighted when the show connected with audiences and ran for over 400 performances.

Berlin wanted to stage an annual revue, as Ziegfeld did, so he immediately went to work on the second edition. Thirteen months later, the second *Music Box Revue* opened with Charlotte Greenwood, former Ziegfeld Girl Grace LaRue, John Steel, and William Gaxton. Berlin had also signed the comic team of Bobby Clark and Paul McCullough in London for their Broadway debut in the show. Clark, with his greasepaint glasses, was one of the stage's great funnymen, and would go on to shows by the Gershwins, Cole Porter, and Vernon Duke. Dancer Ruth Page made her only Broadway appearance in this edition as well. Short created wonderful stage effects. For example, in the "Diamond Horseshoe" number, John Steel sang while a showgirl walked upstage, her rhinestone-covered gown gradually enveloping the stage and turning it into a dazzling curtain of "white fire." Berlin wrote "Pack Up Your Sins and Go to the Devil," which featured impersonators of some of Broadway's great singers and dancers descending by a hidden elevator to "Satan's Palace"; "Lady of the Evening," which he once considered his favorite tune; and "Crinoline Days." The show was another hit, running for 330 performances.

The shows were successful in part because they were smart, funny, and urbane. The country was starting to change from the genteel world centered on agrarian culture to the bustling world of the city, defined by New York. It is easy to see that in a city known as "the melting pot" the division between highbrow culture and popular amusement was disappearing in the Jazz Age. The social classes discovered they enjoyed much of the same type of entertainment, fueled in part by illicit speakeasies, the aftermath of World War I, and the spread of popular entertainment. Some of Berlin's closest friends at the time were part of the Algonquin Round Table, and their sparkling wit is evident in many of these songs, even in his ballads. The wordplays of the songs of this period such as "Lazy" and "All Alone" are some of his deftest creations.

Preparing his two previous editions, Berlin had gone to Atlantic City; he went again for several weeks to work on the third. He returned with a valise full of songs for the next revue, which opened exactly two years after the first. The show is now best remembered for the special effects Short dreamed up for the song "An Orange

Irving Berlin knew how important casting was to the success of a revue. Before he produced his own at the Music Box, he had worked with such indelible performers as Bert Williams, Marilyn Miller, W. C. Fields, Will Rogers, and Fanny Brice. When assembling his own casts, he took equal care with the singers and dancers as he did with the comedians whose antics were as memorable as the songs. (Clockwise from top left) comedian Bobby Clark with Fanny Brice; modern dancer Ruth Page; Claire Luce; dancer and choreographer Carl Randall and Ula Sharon; tenor John Steel and soprano Grace Moore; and comedian Hal Barton.

Neysa McMein's vivid portrait of Berlin. Her studio was a salon for members of the Algonquin Round Table.

Grove in California," in which devices under patrons' seats emitted an orange scent while John Steel and soon-to-be-opera-star Grace Moore sang. Berlin also travestied opera again in a burlesque that featured performers singing "Yes, We Have No Bananas" (written in 1923 by Frank Silver and Irving Cohn) instead of the great opera roles they were costumed for. While no real hit came from the original revue score, six months into the run Berlin interpolated his own "What'll I Do?," which became an overnight sensation.

By the fourth and final *Music Box Revue,* Berlin had learned that supplying a show with a score every year was hard work. As he wrote the woman who would become his second wife, Ellin Mackay, "the thrill of the *Music Box* has gone and now it has become a job that I love most when it's finished." Hassard Short had left to stage his own eponymous revues at the Ritz Theatre, so Berlin brought in John Murray Anderson, who had made a name for himself staging the very successful *Greenwich Village Follies.* They had hoped to open by Thanksgiving 1924,

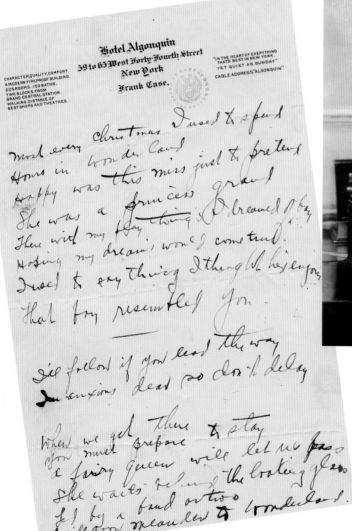

In the early twenties Berlin was a frequent guest of the writers and critics who met at the Algonquin Hotel on Forty-fourth Street, just around the corner from the Music Box. Berlin spent enough time at the hotel to write lyrics there, including the "Alice in Wonderland" number in his 1924 *Music Box Revue.* The wit of the Algonquin banter found its way into Berlin's lyrics, which grew richer as the decade progressed. The Round Table group also became professional colleagues. Berlin scored shows for George S. Kaufman and later for Robert Sherwood. He wrote for a Heywood Broun revue, and hired Robert Benchley to perform at the Music Box, giving the writer a second career as an actor. Alexander Woollcott (seen above with Berlin) wrote the first Berlin biography in 1925.

Berlin twice turned to Lewis Carroll's *Alice in Wonderland* for production numbers in revues. The first was in 1916's *The Century Girl,* a nostalgic song introduced by Hazel Dawn and Irving Fisher. In 1924's *Music Box Revue,* the book and its classic John Tenniel illustrations were brought to life (below) as the Brox sisters invited the audience to "come along with Alice." Berlin referred to it as "Your Alice in Wonderland" when he wrote to Ellin and said it was his "favorite." He filmed this version in *Puttin' on the Ritz* (1930).

to have it and send it on to you — Also, when the show is on, I will send you all the music and notices — The latter may not be so good because the critics haven't had a chance to talk it over with you before writing what they think — In any case — I am sure "Your Alice in Wonderland" will be one of the best numbers — It's my favorite and has turned out better than I expected — By the way — I haven't heard a thing about Lillie Havemeyers arrival so I guess she didn't sail after all — Do you know anything about it? I would love to ask her to the opening if she were here — And now — Good-night dear — I have a date

"All Alone," "Remember," and "Always," three of Berlin's greatest songs from the 1920s—standards that, because of their beautiful melodies and heartfelt lyrics, are still sung today—were all inspired by one woman: Ellin Mackay. Throughout his life, Berlin always denied that his songs were autobiographical, but in these cases it simply was not true. Berlin wrote these songs of longing and love for the woman who would be his wife of sixty-two years and the mother of his three daughters. He wrote them, in part, because he thought he might never see her again.

They met at a dinner party in the spring of 1924, by chance, as he had been a last-minute replacement. Ellin, daughter of multimillionaire Clarence Mackay, told the smart-looking songwriter she liked his song "What Shall I Do?" Berlin corrected her; it was "What'll I Do?," but he joked, to make her feel better, that "Where grammar is concerned, I can always use a little help." After the party, he invited her to join him at Jimmy Kelly's, his old employer, who had moved his operations from Union Square to Greenwich Village. Soon there were other dates at the Astor Roof and Coney Island (with Cole Porter). Berlin's ragtime craze had metamorphosed into the Jazz Age, and class distinctions had fallen by the wayside—but not in the world of Clarence Mackay, who did not envision a Russian Jewish immigrant from the Lower East Side, no matter how wealthy or successful, as a potential son-in-law.

When Mackay found out about the romance, he did everything he could to stop it. He hired private investigators to dig up dirt on Berlin, he barred Ellin from seeing him, and eventually sent her to Europe for six months in the hope that she would forget him. If anything, the separation only intensified their feelings. It was during this hiatus that Berlin wrote, "My life is very lonely/For I want you only" in "All Alone" and the self-pitying concern, "And after I learned to care a lot/You promised that you'd forget me not/But you forgot..." in "Remember."

Mackay then arranged for his daughter to spend the summer out West, in an attempt to break the bond between the pair, but the connection between the songwriter and the debutante grew stronger. Berlin, as usual, said it simply: "I'll be loving you always."

In January 1926 Berlin decided he was going to marry Ellin immediately or not at all, so they trooped down to City Hall for a marriage license with two friends as witnesses. Berlin was so nervous that he forgot his wallet and had to borrow the necessary two dollars. The emerging national press, the same media that spread the tales of Berlin's success, now turned his marriage into a scandal. Mackay did indeed cut off his daughter (although she received money from a trust set up by her mother), so Berlin gave her the copyright to the hit she had inspired, "Always," as a wedding gift. Relentless reporters did everything in their

FLORENCE VANDAMM
N.Y.

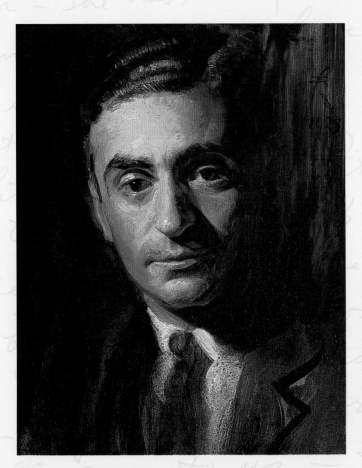

power to fan the flames of controversy, fabricating heated exchanges between Berlin and his father-in-law, as well as the story that one of the newlyweds would convert to the other's religion. Irving and Ellin tried to escape to Atlantic City, a place where Berlin had always found the solitude he needed to write. But reporters and photographers followed them there. Soon they were off to Europe for a six-month honeymoon visiting with friends in Paris.

....

OPPOSITE: Berlin on the roof of his home on Forty-sixth Street, in 1925, the year he was courting Ellin.

ABOVE, LEFT: An oil portrait of Berlin painted in Palm Beach by an unknown Russian artist, ca. 1927.

ABOVE, RIGHT: A portrait of young Ellin Mackay that always hung in the Berlins' homes for their more than sixty years of marriage.

Eventually the press found other gossip and left the Berlins alone. They returned to New York in September 1926, and Berlin picked up where he had left off, writing his classic "Blue Skies" by the end of the year. He and Ellin started married life at the Warwick Hotel before moving to his house at 29 West Forty-sixth Street with their baby daughter, Mary Ellin.

After the death of Mackay's mother, father and daughter shared a moment at the funeral, and slowly the ice began to melt. While Mackay and Berlin were never close, they both understood they loved Ellin, and that Ellin loved them.

Berlin worked very hard, day and night, but he always had time for his family. Despite being surrounded by beautiful women on Broadway and in Hollywood, Berlin never strayed, or was even rumored to have strayed. Ellin remained the love of his life.

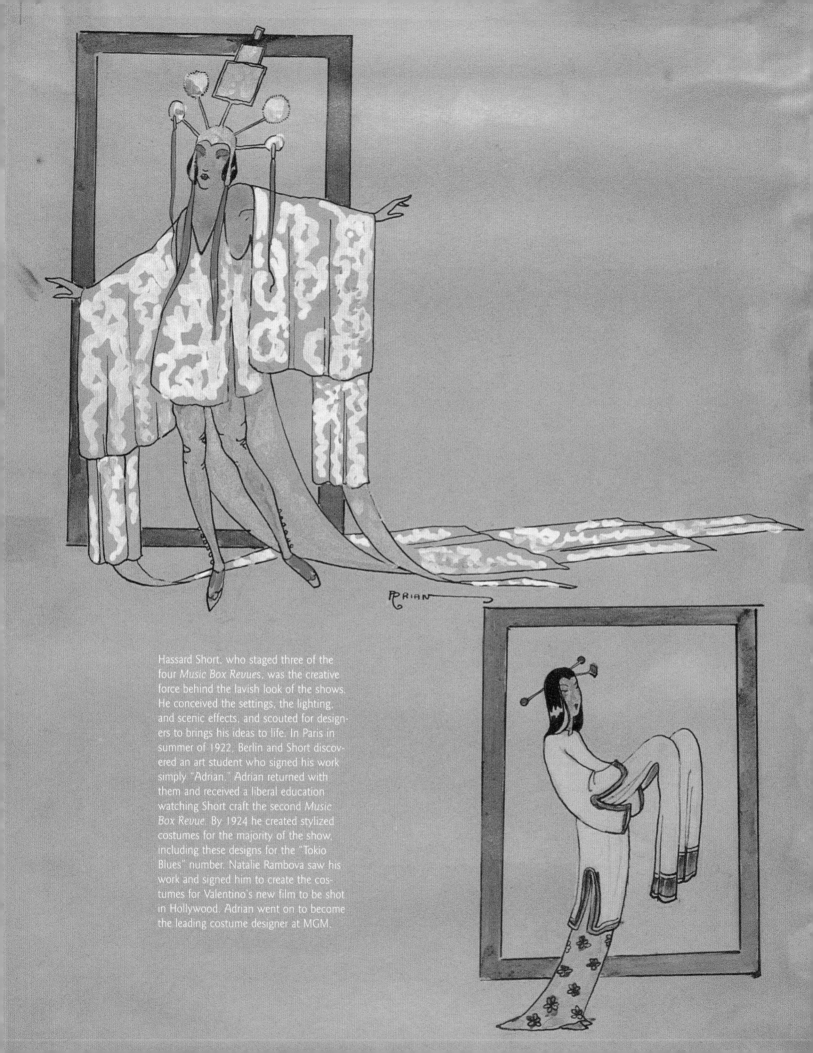

Hassard Short, who staged three of the four *Music Box Revues*, was the creative force behind the lavish look of the shows. He conceived the settings, the lighting, and scenic effects, and scouted for designers to brings his ideas to life. In Paris in summer of 1922, Berlin and Short discovered an art student who signed his work simply "Adrian." Adrian returned with them and received a liberal education watching Short craft the second *Music Box Revue*. By 1924 he created stylized costumes for the majority of the show, including these designs for the "Tokio Blues" number. Natalie Rambova saw his work and signed him to create the costumes for Valentino's new film to be shot in Hollywood. Adrian went on to become the leading costume designer at MGM.

but by the beginning of November, Berlin wrote Ellin, "the rehearsals have been on for a week and a half and they are very much the 'three-ring circus'—the show (as usual) started out to be small and simple and has grown so large that it frightens me a bit." Harris and Berlin had again raided Ziegfeld's stable, this time recruiting Fanny Brice and Carl Randall, and brought back performers such as Clark and McCullough and the Brox Sisters, who had appeared in the previous edition. Again Berlin's score introduced no smash hits, although he did have success with "Who?" and "Tell Her in the Springtime." Anderson's effects were not as startling as Short's but almost every review mentioned how his lighting changed the faces of the chorus from white to black in "The Bandana Ball" number. As Berlin wrote to Ellin a month after the show opened, "Mr. Harris and I saw Saturday night's performance and agreed it is the best *Music Box Revue* since the first. In any case we're doing the biggest business we ever did and that is the final criticism and proof."

The proliferation of revues lessened the impact of many of them. The following season, Berlin worked with George Kaufman on *The Cocoanuts,* a "book show" for the Marx Brothers. Despite his attempts over the next three decades to resurrect them, there would never be another *Music Box Revue.*

The last revue that Berlin contributed to in the 1920s was the *Ziegfeld Follies of 1927.* He supplied the entire score, yet Joseph Urban, at the height of his powers with his elaborate sets, overwhelmed almost everything else in the production. Ruth Etting introduced "Shaking the Blues Away," a hit again two decades later when featured in the film *Easter Parade.* According to Ziegfeld's daughter, her father offered Berlin the chance to write the score for *Show Boat,* but Berlin did not see any commercial material in it. The year 1927, though, would be the turning point in American entertainment. *Show Boat* would usher in the era of the integrated musical, and the film premiere of *The Jazz Singer* gave movies a chance to be heard.

As a song that was dropped from the Boston tryout of the *Ziegfeld Follies of 1927* declared, "You Have to Have 'It' in Hollywood." With a string of Broadway successes to his name as composer and producer, and a thriving music publishing business of his own, Berlin definitely had "It." So Berlin went west.

Mary Ellin was the first child of Irving and Ellin Berlin. Born on Thanksgiving, November 25, 1926, she made the newlyweds, back from a six-month honeymoon in Europe, a family. As Berlin's bachelor apartment was turned into a family home, the songwriter worked on a new song for his daughter, the ever-optimistic "Blue Skies." Berlin's evident joy in his marriage, his daughter, and seemingly life in general, is captured in the lyrics and the melody.

That winter, perhaps influenced by Mary Ellin's arrival, Berlin wrote "Russian Lullaby," in which a mother sings to her child "Rock-a-bye, my baby/Somewhere there may be/A land that's free/For you and me/And a Russian lullaby." The song seemed to bring together his past and his daughter's future in a lovely, lilting tune.

In 1994, Mary Ellin's insightful and affectionate book recalling life with her father was published. *Irving Berlin: A Daughter's Memoir* gives the reader a vivid picture of life in the Berlin household.

Irving Berlin and Hollywood have been linked ever since the movies began to make sound. *The Jazz Singer* is considered the first "talkie," but it was Berlin who made the movies sing when Jolson's character crooned "Blue Skies" to his mother in the film. In the wake of the film's success, Berlin went to Hollywood with the first migration of songwriters. Soon his songs were in films by all the major studios, with Mary Pickford, Laurel and Hardy, Douglas Fairbanks, and Joan Crawford. As a publisher, Berlin saw that movies, like the revues he had left behind, provided the right visual component to introduce a song, but to a much wider audience.

He tried to see that each film song was placed to its best advantage. Berlin also recognized the potential of animation, and allowed several songs to be made into animated shorts by the fledgling Fleischer Studios. Yet many of his early film efforts were unsuccessful, and only two long-lasting hits, "Puttin' on the Ritz" and "Let Me Sing and I'm Happy," come from this period. By the end of his first five years in the movie colony, movie musicals were considered "box office poison." But the period did provide an invaluable education that allowed Berlin to conquer the medium only a few years later.

Filming the title song of 1930's *Puttin' on the Ritz*.

HOLLYWOOD
1927-1931

Berlin Goes Hollywood

1927

1928

1929

October 6 *The Jazz Singer* (Warner Brothers) is released.

November 17 Samuel Goldwyn's film *The Awakening* is released starring Vilma Banky, featuring as its theme "Marie," later a Tommy Dorsey hit.

January 22 D. W. Griffith's *Lady of the Pavements* (United Artists) premieres. Primarily a silent picture, in it Lupe Velez sings Berlin's "Where Is the Song of Songs for Me?" at three different climaxes.

March 30 *Coquette* (United Artists) is released with Berlin's title song for Mary Pickford's first "talkie." Pickford wins an Academy Award for her performance, but the film is not a success.

1930

1931

August 3 *Little Accident* (Universal), starring Douglas Fairbanks, Anita Page, and Zasu Pitts, features Berlin music.

December 29 *Reaching for the Moon* (United Artists), based on a Berlin scenario, is released. All but one of its five songs are deleted before the picture is released and the title tune is only played under the credits.

May 9 An animated short of *Alexander's Ragtime Band* by the Fleischer Studio is released.

August 15 Laurel and Hardy's "talkie" *Pardon Us* (MGM) is released with Berlin music.

December 26 An animated short of *Russian Lullaby* is released.

1929   1930

May 3 The film *The Cocoanuts* (Paramount) premieres with three additional songs by Berlin.

July 8 The Brox Sisters sing "How Many Times?" in *The Time, the Place and the Girl* (Vitaphone—Warner Brothers).

August 20 *Hallelujah* (MGM), the first major studio all-black musical, is released, featuring two Berlin songs, including "Waiting at the End of the Road."

December 7 *Glorifying the American Girl* (Paramount), a screen hagiography of the *Ziegfeld Follies*, is released, in which Berlin makes a cameo appearance as himself.

February 19 *Puttin' on the Ritz* (United Artists) is released with four songs by Berlin. The title song is the first on film to feature an interracial ensemble.

March 26 *Mammy* (Warners), based on an original script by Berlin titled *Mister Bones*, is released. A story of doomed love on the minstrel circuit, it starred Al Jolson singing five Berlin songs, including "Let Me Sing and I'm Happy."

May 3 Dolores Del Rio sings a few bars of Berlin's 1925 song "Tango Melody" (from *The Cocoanuts*) in *The Bad One* (United Artists).

July 19 "Puttin' on the Ritz" is heard in *Our Blushing Brides* (MGM), starring Joan Crawford.

Irving Berlin visiting Lon Chaney on the set with Jack Cohn, 1928.

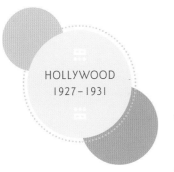

I ASK YOU,
IS THAT NICE?

On April 6, 1929, Mary Pickford's first "talkie," *Coquette,* premiered in New York. As the house lights dimmed, an amplifier blew a fuse and most of the film's sound, including its Irving Berlin title theme song, was barely audible. For Berlin, it was an apt metaphor for his experiences in the new medium.

His film career started with promise. As early as 1919, Berlin had recognized that the movies were an outlet for his songs. Studios understood that a "tie-in" with a popular song could be valuable promotion for a film. Over eight years, Berlin published a handful of songs with covers linked to films. With the success of *The Jazz Singer* in October 1927, the industry struggled to change its silents in production to "all talking–all singing" features. Berlin, with his twenty-year reputation unmatched, was one of the first songwriters Hollywood turned to.

In the past, Warners had provided musical soundtracks so that a theater could show silent movies without hiring piano players or orchestras to accompany them. In *The Jazz Singer,* the studio presented Jolson's songs in synchronized sound as well. This allowed people around the country to hear what New York audiences had enjoyed for over a decade: Al Jolson singing several numbers, including Berlin's "Blue Skies." Originally his solo was to have been "When I Lost You," but the studio wanted a fresher hit. "Blue Skies" had stolen the show in December 1926 when it had been interpolated into the opening night score of Rodgers and Hart's *Betsy.* For *The Jazz Singer* it was the ideal song for Jolson's character to sing as an example of his new Broadway music. It also demonstrated how the new medium could convey an intimacy not found on the stage. Through close-ups, here between a mother and a son, film offered a better view than any front-row seat. When Jolson talked and sang in the sequence, the idea of the "talkies" was born.

The Broadway musical itself was changing as taking pictures came in. Revues were starting to show signs of age. As Berlin himself discovered, repeatedly coming up with new ways to stage spectacle, song, and satire was

Mary Pickford and Johnny Mack Brown break into talking pictures in *Coquette* in 1929.

Berlin in a contemplative moment on a movie set.

The two faces of Al Jolson's Jakie Rabinowitz in *The Jazz Singer.* At top the cantor's son, a dutiful boy, and below in blackface, a Broadway sensation. At lower right, Jolson takes in a few holes with Berlin in 1928.

OPPOSITE: Warner Brothers thought the scene when Jakie Rabinowitz sings "Blue Skies" to his mother was so important that it was immortalized on the film's poster.

exhausting, and the crowd and critics began to feel the same. Ziegfeld understood this, and shelved his annual revue after its 1927 edition. On December 26, 1927, he opened *Show Boat,* which played 532 performances and changed the whole equation. An integrated musical with songs that were written not only for the character but as a way of advancing an intelligent story was what audiences wanted. Even after the success of *Show Boat,* Berlin's interest in Hollywood may have caused him to put off pursuing this new development. Before *Show Boat* opened, he had collaborated with actor James Gleason on *Mr. Bones,* a stage musical set in a traveling minstrel show. The script became the basis for the film *Mammy* in 1930.

Music in films maintained a status quo for Berlin, reflecting the Broadway tradition of interpolations and revues. There was more story in films than in revues, but the conventional wisdom was that musical numbers required a performance setting, which limited the actors' roles to singers or dancers. Consequently, songs were frequently unrelated to the story line. Berlin's reputation and friendship with Joe Schenck provided him access to all the top producers and studios, and he found placing songs was fairly easy. In just the next three

ABOVE: Every year for more than twenty years, there was a new George S. Kaufman comedy on Broadway. Kaufman's plays won two Pulitzer Prizes for drama, and his comedies are among the few from the 1920s and 1930s that are still revived regularly today. After his work on *The Cocoanuts*, he became one of Broadway's top directors. He directed Berlin and Moss Hart's *Face the Music* in 1932.

RIGHT: Berlin accompanying Irving Thalberg and his wife, Norma Shearer, to a premiere ca. 1930.

OPPOSITE: Groucho Marx steals another scene in the film version of *The Cocoanuts*.

years, he oversaw the adaptation of a stage hit, had his music featured in twenty films, and wrote two complete film scores.

Berlin's next significant work on screen was the film version of *The Cocoanuts* in 1929. The 1925 stage production for the Marx Brothers was a trying experience for librettist George S. Kaufman, because the comedians were pathological ad libbers. Like dealing with the Marxes themselves, Berlin found his work on the show became "topsy turvy. My well-laid score was opened up and I wrote new songs, new lyrics, and eventually we had an entirely different production than had been planned." The show was a hit, but a Marx Brothers hit, not a Berlin one, with no memorable songs. The film, with one new song, proved no different.

As the popularity of musical films increased, studios paid handsomely for Tin Pan Alley songs and soon purchased music publishers to own the songs rather than pay a royalty for them. Soon songwriters were on the West Coast instead of West Twenty-eighth Street. Berlin's company held out against the gold rush, although he did open an office in Hollywood in the 1920s. He started to supply story treatments in 1929 with defined placements for his songs in order to better position them for success in the film and with the music-buying public.

ABOVE: William Auerbach Levy's drawing of the Marx Brothers in the stage production of *The Cocoanuts.*

RIGHT: Groucho Marx and Margaret Dumont in the stage production of *The Cocoanuts* (1925).

"THE COCOANUTS" – 1929
MILTON (ZEPPO) - MARX   JULIUS ("GROUCHO") MARX
LEONARD ("CHICO") MARX - ARTHUR ("HARPO") MARX

The Cocoanuts starred the Marx Brothers in a comedy about the Florida land boom in the 1920s. In it, Groucho describes a location to Harpo and Chico, saying, "Now here is a little peninsula and here is a viaduct leading over to the mainland." To which Chico replies, "Why a duck?"

Puttin' on the Ritz (1930) was Berlin's idea originally. He wanted to film the story of Tin Pan Alley on location in New York. The film soon metamorphosed into the kind of typical backstage picture that the studios were churning out regularly. Harry Richman plays an egotistical performer who goes blind by drinking bad whisky and is saved by the love of Joan Bennett. Berlin's title tune would be an instant classic, but it was lost in a film whose plot already seemed out of date. The studio insisted that Berlin be one of several songwriters on the picture. He wrote two new tunes and revived the "Alice in Wonderland" production number from the *Music Box Revue.* On the eve of the film's premiere, Berlin wrote to his friend and partner Max Winslow at his office, "The 'Vagabond' song ["There's Danger in Your Eyes, Cherie," by Pete Wendling and Jack Meskill] is done three times, but you know how we both felt about this song. Frankly, I am little bit ashamed to have it in the picture with such rhymes as 'jewel'ry' and 'foole'ry' and 'legion' and 'religion.' It was a mistake at the outset to stand for any interpolations, and I am certain, as I said before, they would have had a more consistent set of numbers had they left it to me."

But he had more worries. While filming the "Alice" number, he learned of the 1929 stock market crash. Berlin had two decades' worth of earnings tied up in the market. "I was scared. I had had all the money I wanted for the rest of my life. Then all of a sudden I didn't." With a wife and child, Berlin had come to rely partly on his publishing income, especially since his pace for composing had slowed from the frantic years of revues. Now he felt that "I had taken it easy and

Some Reasons for the "S. R. O." Sign at the Ziegfeld Follies

Soon after the film debuted, Al Hirschfeld captured Harry Richman (upper left) singing "Puttin' on the Ritz" in the *Ziegfeld Follies* on Broadway.

gone soft and wasn't too certain I could get going again." To his publishing partner Saul Bornstein, who ran his office in New York, he wrote, "I do believe that the regular music business is over, even for those with picture connections." He felt confident that his upcoming film music would help for a while, but concluded "the day of the very big hits is over; unless conditions change, it is again entirely up to the merit of the song." While Berlin was shaken by the crash, he would soon incorporate it into a scenario, *Love in a Cottage,* which he was writing for Joe Schenck.

In the meantime, Berlin had reason for confidence. He had a great "set up," as he often referred to his film deals. He reunited with Al Jolson in a story, *Mister Bones,* that he had cowritten about the life of a minstrel troupe, now titled *Mammy.* Berlin felt black-faced minstrel shows were a quintessential American experience, and he set a tragic love story against this backdrop. Jolson was among the biggest draws in movies and Berlin wrote him a song that would become both a hit and a signature number for Jolson, "Let Me Sing and I'm Happy." The other four songs and the film itself did not find an audience. Moviegoers were tired of musicals, and, it was reported, they approached box offices asking, "It's not a musical, is it?" Film musicals were going through a shakeout, and *Mammy* was the first Jolson film to lose money.

Berlin wanted to return to New York, but felt duty-bound to honor his commitment to Joe Schenck for *Love in a Cottage.* This was the third picture for which Berlin had written the scenario, and he wrote to Max Winslow in February 1930 that he was "very enthusiastic about the story," which he described as a "modern musical comedy, with a good love story. So far, there is nothing heavy in it, and I am trying to keep the atmosphere light." From extant scripts, it appears it was to be an elegant musical farce of the sort that would become the hallmark of Fred Astaire–Ginger Rogers films, but without the dancing. Berlin's concerns about casting were allayed when Douglas Fairbanks and Bebe Daniels were signed. In May he wrote happily to Ellin that he had just composed "the best waltz I've done

In *Mammy,* Jolson played Al Fuller, a minstrel star who is framed for murder when a rival puts real bullets into Fuller's stage gun.

since 'What'll I Do?,' " a song that would become the new title of the film *Reaching for the Moon.* By the end of August 1930 script changes had slowed production, and although Berlin still felt it would be a "great picture," he wrote Bornstein, "It's pretty hard for me to stir up any enthusiasm, because I have been on it too long and it's really gotten on my nerves."

Berlin must have seen the picture slipping out of his control. Director Edmund Goudling had decided that the film would be better without music and slowly deleted all of the songs, many of which were integrated into the plot. The only number remaining was "When the Folks High Up Do the Mean Low Down," sung by a very young Bing Crosby in a performance setting that has nothing to do with the story of the film. The title waltz is used as underscoring on the opening credits, which stated that the movie was based on a "story with music by Irving Berlin."

The assembly-line production of Hollywood films had ground down Berlin's self-confidence. He wrote his song-publishing partner Saul Bornstein in 1930 that "I have been away from New York and the office so long that my judgment on my

Jolson and company present an authentic blackface minstrel show in *Mammy.*

IRVING BERLIN'S SHOW BUSINESS

own stuff may not be one hundred percent." Back in New York, despite nearly twenty-five years in the business, Berlin began to believe that he had lost his touch, and consequently the pleasure he received from songwriting. For the next two years in New York he published very little of his own music, believing that the public was not interested. He did decide to challenge himself by writing the score for a new Broadway show, *Face the Music,* but even its success did not completely alleviate his sense of ennui.

Max Winslow waited until Berlin left for a vacation in the Adirondacks to bring Rudy Vallee a Berlin song that the composer had felt unworthy:"Say It Isn't So." The song's sentiments mirrored those of the singer, who was separating from his wife. Singing it for the first time on his weekly radio show, Vallee delivered it with such emotion that listeners around the country were touched. It became a hit, and people bought both the sheet music and Vallee's record. Vallee credited the song with saving his marriage. Berlin, like many ASCAP members, was suspicious of radio and had fought to receive royalties for the airplay of his work. Now radio had given him what he needed most: a hit. The song's success made him think of other songs in his "trunk" still unpublished. From "To My Mammy," from *Mammy*—"a true horror," according to Berlin later—he lifted phrases to create one of his most enduring standards, "How Deep Is the Ocean?" Hollywood had given him an "inferiority complex," but a couple of hits restored his joy in writing music as thousands cheered.

ABOVE: Alex Gard's caricature of Rudy Vallee for Sardi's. Vallee had two important Berlin recordings, "Say It Isn't So" in 1932, and the Oscar-nominated "I Poured My Heart into a Song" from *Second Fiddle* (1939).

BELOW: Douglas Fairbanks Jr., as a successful stockbroker, woos aviator Bebe Daniels before the stock market crash in *Reaching for the Moon* (1930).

When Berlin returned to New York in December 1930, he was dejected by the reception of his last four years of work and thought that he might finally be, after a quarter century of songwriting, washed up. So the forty-two-year-old Berlin connected with the fair-haired boy of Broadway, George Kaufman's latest playwrighting partner, the twenty-six-year-old Moss Hart. The Berlin-Hart collaborations restored the songwriter's confidence and reputation as a hit-maker, and the palpable excitement that Berlin must have felt in writing these songs can still be felt today. The two shows, *Face the Music* and *As Thousands Cheer,* topical satires that delighted Depression audiences, signaled both the end of the lavish Broadway revue and the beginning of a streamlined version. *Face the Music* parodied the excess of Ziegfeld, while *As Thousands Cheer* used simple elements to create a unified revue. Three years before the Federal Theatre Project debuted their innovative *Living Newspaper Unit,* Berlin and Hart had brought the newspaper to life in *As Thousands Cheer.* Both shows put Berlin back in the headlines.

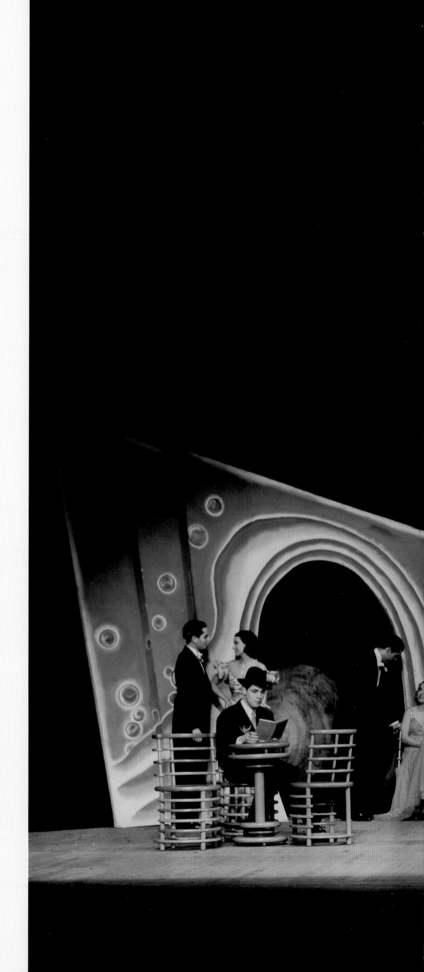

Albert Johnson's modern sets gave a fresh look to *Face the Music.*

BROADWAY
1932-1934

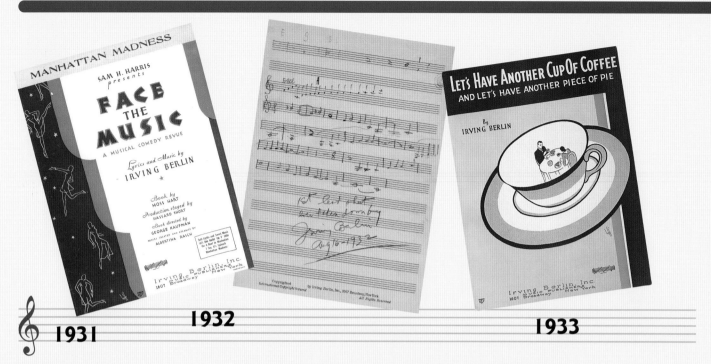

1931

1932

1933

Summer Berlin starts work on *Face the Music*.

February 17 *Face the Music* opens on Broadway. The musical satire runs 165 performances before going out on a national tour. After twenty-five years of songwriting, Berlin writes his first lead sheet (above).

Fall Berlin starts work on *As Thousands Cheer*. Hart goes to Hollywood. Berlin visits and in ten days they sketch out the idea of the show and the first act.

January 31 *Face the Music* returns to Broadway for 31 performances.

In this scene from the show-within-a-show in *The Rhinestones of 1932*, Berlin and Hart parodied the revue in *Face the Music*. The duo reimagined the revue in *As Thousands Cheer*.

1933

May Berlin and Hart go to Bermuda to work on the second act of *As Thousands Cheer* undistracted.

Summer Hart spends time in Skowhegan, Maine, at actress Jean Dixon's home, finishing the second act.

1934

September 30 Berlin and Hart reinvent the revue in *As Thousands Cheer*, which lives up to its name during its 400 performances. When Dorothy Stone replaces Marilyn Miller in the topical show, reviewers all claim that the show still retains its freshness, although each claims a different sketch seems by now to be out of date.

May Berlin and Hart spend nineteen days at sea on the S.S. *Rex* working on a sequel to *As Thousands Cheer*, to be called *More Cheers*. Although Berlin writes a number of songs, the two decide to shelve the project. Berlin goes to Hollywood and Hart reunites with George Kaufman to write *Merrily We Roll Along*.

1935

February 21 *As Thousands Cheer* opens in London as *Stop Press*.

Newspaper headlines introduced each number in *As Thousands Cheer*. The show's first song dealt with America's all-time great headline "Man Bites Dog."

MANHATTAN
MADNESS

*"It seems like old, and very good times, to have the best musical show in
town with words and music by Irving Berlin."*

Gilbert Seldes, 1932

Revues were dead; Berlin understood that. After
watching them fall ill on Broadway, he saw
them on their deathbed in Hollywood. With the Depression sinking in at all levels
of American society, the idea of a lavish spectacle was beyond the reach of many
producers and audiences. He wanted to work on a "book show," a musical comedy
that would compete head-on with the Young Turks of Broadway: Rodgers and
Hart, the Gershwins, and Cole Porter. For comedy, Berlin knew the fount of writing and staging; it was his former collaborator and Round Table member in good
standing, George S. Kaufman. Kaufman, busy with a new Gershwin show, suggested Moss Hart, a young playwright with whom he had collaborated on the
Hollywood satire *Once in a Lifetime,* a huge hit at the Music Box when it opened in
September 1930. Although Kaufman collaborated with Hart on the play, directed
the production, and played a role in it, on opening night he told the audience, in
one of the few curtain speeches he ever made, that the play was "eighty percent
Moss Hart."

Like Berlin, Hart had come from an impoverished background, but at the
other end of New York: the Bronx. After seeing Kaufman and Ring Lardner's
comedy *June Moon,* Hart knew he wanted to be a playwright, and worked tirelessly
but unsuccessfully until he read about the panic in Hollywood over the arrival of
"talkies." He crafted a comedy about three vaude-
villians who head west, passing themselves off as
voice teachers. He submitted the play to Sam
Harris, who liked it enough to think it would make
a great musical. Although the offer was tempting,

....
Edward Steichen captured Hugh
O'Connell and some of his fellow
policemen on the set of *Face
the Music.*

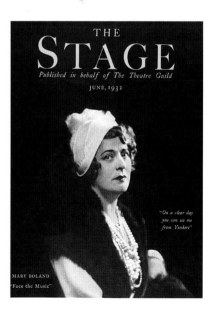

Face the Music was the first musical for
Mary Boland, a twenty-five-year veteran of
the Broadway stage.

Hart refused to add music. When Harris suggested Kaufman as a collaborator, the young man was thrilled. They worked on *Once in a Lifetime* for six months, tried it out of town, and it flopped. They revised it and the show flopped again. On closing night Kaufman told Hart the show was his to do with what he wanted and he hoped the next effort would be more successful. Over the weekend Hart feverishly reworked the show and burst into Kaufman's office on Monday morning and practically performed the show himself to demonstrate to Kaufman where it needed work. Kaufman decided to give it another try, and a playwrighting team was born.

After the success of *Once in a Lifetime,* Hart moved his family, much as Berlin had done for his mother with his early success, to a new home in the Bronx. He soon decamped for Hollywood, but again like Berlin and the characters in his own show, he became depressed at how movies were made. Although Hart had expressed disdain for musical comedy when Sam Harris had suggested it, when the offer came from Irving Berlin, Hart could not say no.

Berlin was nervous. He knew that on Broadway a songwriter was "only as good as his last show," and his 1927 *Follies* had not been particularly memorable. Yet he plunged into new territory, writing and rewriting material over more than a year to

BELOW: Classically trained dancer Albertina Rasch had her own troupe when she choreographed *Face the Music.* She incorporated steps from ballet, fused with a modern style, as shown here from the show's second act.

OPPOSITE: Katherine Carrington in a lavish costume created by Weld for the revue parody *The Rhinestones* (1932).

craft a sharp, satiric show based on New York's investigation of its popular, partying mayor, Jimmy Walker. Berlin liked Walker, and had even written tribute verse and dedicated a song to support him, but the massive corruption that had transpired under his watch was the stuff of a satirist's dream. In what would eventually be called *Face the Music,* the Depression has forced the "Morgans and the Whitneys and all the other big shots" to eat in automats; Ethel Barrymore is reduced to playing on the same bill with Albert Einstein, Al Jolson, and Eddie Cantor at the Palace, and eating lunch for a nickel. The only people with money are the policemen who put their bribes and kickbacks into little tin boxes, but they need to hide it from investigators. One character, the producer Hal Reisman (a stand-in for Ziegfeld), provides a sure way to hide the money. Reisman has them invest in a guaranteed flop, a lavish revue, *The Rhinestones of 1932,* showing that Mel Brooks's *The Producers* was not the first instance of a show based on this scheme. The plan works as intended, but when Reisman takes the policemen's suggestions to add nudity and off-color jokes to the show, it becomes a hit, earning everyone some honestly made profits. The show's convoluted plot allowed Hart's acid pen to skewer dozens of topical subjects.

Berlin wrote a stunning collection of what one reviewer called "typical, tantalizing" numbers for his Broadway comeback. Included were production numbers such as the *Follies* parody "My Beautiful Rhinestone Girl" which was played against a shimmering Venetian set encrusted with faux jewels and satiric songs such as "I Say It's Spinach (and the Hell with It)" and the finale, "Investigation." But the show's ballads became standards: "Soft Lights and Sweet Music" and "Let's Have Another Cup of Coffee."

The mix of Hart's barbs and Berlin's music, presented with modern sets and costumes, delighted both audiences and critics. As good as it was, though, the show had the misfortune of opening six weeks after the Gershwin/Kaufman musical landmark *Of Thee I Sing,* to which it was constantly compared by the critics. "*Face the Music* tries to do for show business and the Seabury

Andrew Tombes, Katherine Carrington, and J. Harold Murray.

The title of Berlin's Broadway comeback was in flux almost until the Philadelphia opening. It was originally advertised there as *Louder and Funnier* before becoming *Face the Music.* Below are some of the titles considered and rejected before the show's opening.

Nickels and Dimes	Off the Beat
This Town of Ours	Blue Angels
Manhattan	Brass Buttons
Manhattan	Hullabaloo
Madness	Round the Corner
Manhattan Mirrors	Stand Up and
Manhattan Nights	Cheer
Good Old Gotham	No Left Turn
Gotham Gleanings	High Lights
The Big Town	Wings over
Curtain	Broadway
Curtain Going Up	Happy New Year
Lights	Grand Slam
Footlights	Sing a Song of
Standing Room	Sixpence
Only	Crying Out Loud
Flat Feet and Foot-	Louder and
lights	Funnier

FACE THE MUSIC

● ● ● Sweet music by Berlin . . . and lights not so soft focused by Moss Hart on a bailiwick and its bailiffs soused with gay corruption. We of the gullible public laugh, in spite of a sharp pain at the thought of our taxes, at one of the liveliest and loveliest musical satires that ever hit Broadway hard. Jean Sargent (middle) sings the torch song. Mary Boland and J. Harold Murray co-star.

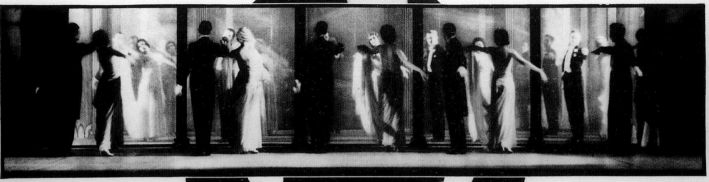

"Soft Lights and Sweet Music" and the illusion of mirrors—in this, the most appealing and romantic of all the scenes.

Confined to "A Roof in Manhattan," one can still dream of Spanish maidens who dance like the Albertina Rasch Girls.

Photo by Vandamm Studio

The reason why cops don't run for President is that they hate to sacrifice such nice private offices as the one above.

"Attractive Costuming in *Face the Music* Contributes to Success of New Musical" was the headline in *Women's Wear*. "Puffed Sleeves, High Necklines, Accented Bustlines Are Typical Details." The elegantly modern costumes by Kiviette and Weld started a vogue in fashion. Ready-to-wear versions were sold at Lord and Taylor. Two of the designs in the advertisement above were from the "On a Roof in Manhattan" number. Judging from their descriptions, they were much more muted in color than the stage creations, which were yellow, orange, and red embroidered with gold thread.

Linda was named after the wife of Cole Porter. Berlin was an early supporter and lifelong friend of Porter's, and the two couples were close. Linda was born February 21, 1932, four days after the opening of *Face the Music* on Broadway. Although the second daughter, she was not the second child of the Berlins. On December 1, 1928, Ellin had given birth to a boy, Irving Berlin, Jr., who died just over three weeks later on Christmas Eve.

Linda's birth coincided with her father's Broadway comeback and his successful return to Hollywood, where he worked for much of the thirties. These events, coupled with his two and one-half years with *This Is the Army*, meant that Berlin was not much of a presence in Linda's childhood. Though she followed her father's work, it was only after taking up the research on *The Complete Lyrics of Irving Berlin* (coedited with Robert Kimball), published in 2001, that she fully appreciated the range of his work, she has said.

Don Freeman

Behind the Scenes in "Face the Music"

Showing the elegance to which the rhinestone girls are accustomed even off stage at the New Amsterdam

A few of the chorus emerging into the patio of the Castle in Spain as they are seen by the spot-light engineers in the revue at the New Amsterdam

Civic Corruption Frivolous

The courtroom investigation of improper political practices at the close of "Face the Music"

From "Facing the Music"

The New Berlin Revue

Joseph Macauly, Katherine Carrington, Hugh O'Connell, Mary Boland (and friend), Andrew Toombes and J. Harold Murray as they will be seen at the New Amsterdam Wednesday

Don Freeman was a student of John Sloan who sketched his subjects in every part of New York City. In the artist-illustrator tradition of Everett Shinn and Reginald Marsh, Freeman supported himself with drawings of life in the theater district, both on stage and off. He may be the only artist who was "backstage-struck," fascinated almost as much with the world of stagehands, doormen, dressers, and ushers as with the performers. His pictorial reporting appeared in *The New York Times, The Herald Tribune, The Christian Science Monitor,* and *Life.* From February to June 1932, Freeman made his illustrations of *Face the Music.* Over those four months, he would return repeatedly to the theater to show the most elaborate numbers in the production from unusual vantage points.

THE MUSICAL SATIRE, "FACE THE MUSIC," FROM OUT FRONT

Vogue published this collage of on-stage photographs from *Face the Music* in May 1932. Taken by an unknown photographer with a night camera, this series is the only photographic documentation of what the original production actually looked like.

IRVING BERLIN'S SHOW BUSINESS

investigation what *Of Thee I Sing* did for presidential campaigns," was a typical observation in the papers. But for audiences, having two good musical satires that punctured the world of privilege and power was almost too good to be true. As for Berlin, he had a double success, since the Pulitzer Prize–winning *Of Thee I Sing* was playing in his Music Box Theatre. The Depression nevertheless only provided audiences for the show until the end of the season, and Hart and Berlin were encouraged by Sam Harris to build on their success.

Hart had originally envisioned a revue for their first show. Now Berlin returned to the idea, but wanted it to look and feel as modern as his last show. He conceived "the city editor's dream of heaven," a satirical revue based on sections of the newspaper. The varied nature of a newspaper could provide ample fodder for both skits and songs. Berlin took obvious ideas such as the weather report ("Heat Wave"), advice columns ("Lonely Heart"), gossip ("Through a Keyhole"), and of course "The Funnies," and made them witty confections that remain fresh today. Columnist Lucius Beebe quoted Berlin talking of "transmuting a newspaper into terms of the musical stage . . . there are no gratuitously inserted sketches or incidental songs." Each number or skit was announced by a headline projected on a curtain above the stage.

ABOVE: Abe Birnbaum's drawing features some of the headlines from *As Thousands Cheer*, along with portraits of (left to right) Ethel Waters, Clifton Webb, Marilyn Miller (in Webb's buttonhole), and Helen Broderick. Caricature is what this show was all about.

LEFT: Helen Broderick represents America, asked to forgive the debts of "England and Italy and Germany and France" in a scene from *As Thousands Cheer* titled "We'll All Be in Heaven when the Dollar Goes to Hell."

OPPOSITE: For the courtroom finale of *Face the Music*, Mary Boland's Mrs. Meshbesher rode in on a papier-mâché elephant to testify for her husband.

As satiric and sharp as Berlin and Hart had been with New York in *Face the Music,* they were now going national in *As Thousands Cheer,* with stories that happened, or were broadcast, everywhere. Through newspaper syndication, newsreels, and radio, popular culture itself was looking beyond Broadway. As the vogue peaked for caricature that laughed *with* its subjects and not *at* them, Depression audiences wanted to see celebrities as just like themselves. Beebe quoted Berlin saying during the Philadelphia tryouts that "there are some persons, you know, who need no distortion to caricature, and the same is true of much of the world's news. It is satire in itself and has only to be photographically

Mr. Dennis F. O'Brien,
O'Brien, Driscoll & Raftery,
152 West 42nd St.,
New York City.

Oct. 3rd, 1933

Dear Cap:

I have your letter, with copy of Arno's claim. The facts are
as follows:-

I wrote the Society Wedding number as one of the first songs
for "As Thousands Cheer". The idea is based on any one of four
of the oldest stories there are.

The phrase, "They married and went right back to bed", and the
line, "I told my fiancee about it, and she nearly fell out of
bed laughing", have been going the rounds long before Peter Arno
was born. The story of the blushing bride, which was current
during the war and, if I am not mistaken, appeared in one of the
American newspapers, was that of a doughboy in bed with a French
girl, and she says to him, "By God, it's a twelve o'clock! I
must be going, as I'm getting married at one."

Boiling it down, there is nothing particularly new about the
idea that my song is based on. It is the way we do it that
makes it different. I never saw Arno's drawing until last
Friday, when it was said that the actual set the number is
played in resembled his drawing. Both Hazzard Short and the
artist who painted the set saw the drawing with me, and everybody agreed there was no resemblance at all.

Arno, no doubt, based his drawing on the same old stories, and
if it is possible for a cartoonist to illustrate Joe Miller's
Joke Book and copyright them, then he probably has a very good
case. If he and his lawyer intend to go to the bat for this,
I have some information for you that will be very valuable.

I neglected to mention that, in a revue called "Hey Nonny Nonny"
which was produced about two years ago, there was a number called
"Wouldn't It Be Wonderful", and that number, too, was based on
the same stories. As I remember, in that show they too had a
bed with the couple dressing, and going off to the gag line of
"And when we are married, wouldn't it be wonderful."

"Wake up, you mutt! We're getting married today."

The day before *As Thousands Cheer* opened, *The New Yorker* cartoonist Peter Arno had his lawyer send a cease-and-desist letter to Berlin over the "Society Wedding" number, which Arno felt was an infringement of his copyrighted cartoon (top right). Berlin wrote a withering rejection of the claim to his own lawyer (top left) drawing on his show-business knowledge for the gag's history. The scene (below) remained in the show.

OPPOSITE: Irving Berlin and Moss Hart in a photo by Vandamm, ca. 1932.

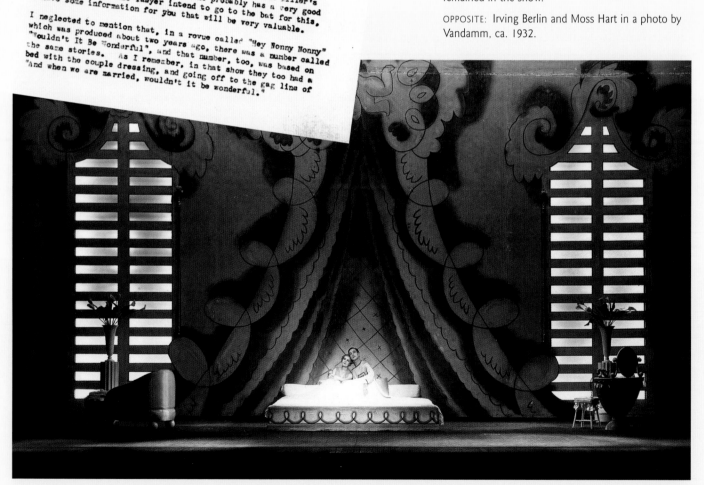

IRVING BERLIN'S SHOW BUSINESS

"We're going to try to inject a serious note into this musical," Berlin told Ethel Waters's managers after hearing her sing "Stormy Weather" at the Cotton Club. The song was "Supper Time," and it stopped the show every night. She made an even bigger hit with "Heat Wave," seen here. In a long and storied career, Waters said, "I never had better material to work with." OPPOSITE: Waters performing (clockwise from top left): "Supper Time," as Josephine Baker in "Harlem on My Mind," and "Heat Wave."

Clifton Webb became a quick-change artist during *As Thousands Cheer*, turning from Douglas Fairbanks, Jr. (bottom left), into John Rockefeller, Sr. (bottom right), in exactly six and one-half minutes. He had only four minutes to change from Rockefeller to a turn-of-the-century beau for the "Easter Parade" finale. He played characters from Gandhi (top left) to a waiter masquerading as Noël Coward (top right). Webb also danced with Marilyn Miller in the show.

reproduced to be the most gorgeous kind of irony." Hart and Berlin gently ribbed celebrities from all walks of life—from Douglas Fairbanks to John D. Rockefeller, from Barbara Hutton to Josephine Baker. When Mahatma Gandhi and the evangelist Aimee Semple McPherson meet during one of Gandhi's hunger strikes, they discuss how much publicity they receive for their work. *The New York Times* critic Brooks Atkinson observed that "Broadway always thinks in terms of Broadway; it finds Broadway motives in every person it satirizes. When it goes through the elaborate ceremony of unmasking a celebrity it only bares the Broadway heart." The show broadened the subjects of its satire, but also softened the sharp edges evident in *Face the Music*. In comparing *As Thousands Cheer* to John Murray Anderson's satiric *Americana,* critic Gilbert Gabriel remarked that the show "manages to say [it] no less sharply, no less caustically. . . but with this one ever-present, ever-saving difference: it says it always five times more merrily. . . . Here, in short, we have it: a come-back to the first principles and best reasons for a brilliant revue, to the delicate jibe and the impudent beauty of moods and goods for which, long ago, the revue idea was born." The Berlin-Hart team had parodied the revue in *Face the Music;* now they revitalized it with *As Thousands Cheer.*

Hassard Short had staged it, and Moss Hart had written the book, but review after review singled out Berlin for praise. He had created a set of numbers that

ABOVE: Letitia Ide and José Limón in "Revolt in Cuba," a dance number from *As Thousands Cheer.*

BELOW: Marilyn Miller on the Toonerville Trolley, with cartoon characters who come to life, in the Irene Sharaff–designed "The Funnies."

ABOVE: Leslie Adams and Helen Broderick as President and Mrs. Herbert Hoover, who are reluctant to leave the White House, in the skit "Franklin D. Roosevelt Inaugurated Tomorrow."

BELOW: The final dress rehearsal of the "Easter Parade" number.

were instantly familiar, yet striking in their composition and lyrics. He had taken obvious ideas and turned them inside out to create sui generis works.

Broadway, in the grip of the Depression, its producers and angels going bankrupt and its bankable stars heading to Hollywood, was shrinking. *As Thousands Cheer* helped to revitalize the theater district when it opened on September 30, 1933, giving audiences and critics alike something to cheer about.

In Broadway billing, the show "starred" Clifton Webb, then known as much as a dancer as an actor; Marilyn Miller, the Ziegfeld beauty and major star of the period; and comedienne Helen Broderick. The show "featured" the African-American singer and actress Ethel Waters in four songs. Despite the starring cast's remarkable combination of comedy, singing, and dancing in lightning-fast costume changes, it was Waters who had the most impact. Berlin had heard Waters at the Cotton Club singing Ted Koehler and Harold Arlen's "Stormy Weather." Waters poured her life of heartbreak into the song, singing "from the depths of the private hell in which I was being crushed and suffocated," she later said.

Berlin got in touch with Waters the next day, because he and Hart had decided to "inject a serious note into this musical." For "Supper Time," the headline was "Unknown Negro Lynched by Frenzied Mob." Waters, dressed in simple clothes, sang the dirge as a woman preparing dinner for her children after learning that her husband has been killed. "If one song can tell the whole tragic history of a race," said Waters, " 'Supper Time' was that song." Waters gave it her all, and was so

exhausted after singing it that a cot was set up backstage so that she could lie down after each performance.

The effect was so powerful that Waters was convinced that the song could never stay in the "gay musical revue." But producer Sam Harris and Berlin believed in it. After its debut at the Wednesday matinee in Philadelphia, Waters remembered "I was called back again and again. I had stopped the show with a type of song never heard before in a revue." It was nearly an impossible act to follow. It stayed in the show.

Soon cast members complained about taking their curtain call with the black actress. There were few, if any, interracial curtain calls on any stage. Berlin decreed that if the cast was unhappy with the situation the easiest solution was to have no curtain call. They all took a bow together the next day, and continued to do it that way throughout the Broadway run and a year of touring.

The show was a smash. Just as Kaufman and the Gershwins missed great success with their first collaboration, it took Berlin and Hart's second satire to capture the zeitgeist. Despite scores that are first-rate, both teams' first efforts were too biting. Both *Of Thee I Sing* and *As Thousands Cheer* have survived because both the book and the music still have the talent to amuse. Although satire, by its topical nature, dates itself, politics and newspapers have remained the same. Hart's vitality had found a kindred spirit. Outside of his work with George Kaufman, Hart never found a better collaborator than Berlin. Now that Berlin had remade the American musical to fit his talents on Broadway, he needed to return to Hollywood and leave his stamp there.

To create the glossy, sepia-toned look for the Act I finale, "Rotogravure Section—Easter Parade on Fifth Avenue—1883," Irene Sharaff, in her Broadway debut, designed the seemingly monochromatic costumes using touches of cool and warm whites among "the bitter chocolate brown, umbers, siennas, and taupes." The cast froze every few lines as if being photographed to translate the idea into theatrical terms.

Albert Johnson

Set designer Albert Johnson was only twenty-two when he had, in the words of Lucius Beebe, "four of the best-known musical successes in the world being presented nightly against his backgrounds: *Three's a Crowd* in Boston, *The Band Wagon* in Chicago, *Waltzes from Vienna* in London, and *Face the Music* in New York's Rialto." Working as a designer for only three years, Johnson had become the top man in his field, and for the next two decades his work would provide the settings for a number of landmark productions, including *Let 'Em Eat Cake, Skin of Our Teeth,* and *Jumbo.*

Johnson got his start in show business the old-fashioned way: he ran away with the circus. Although he wanted to be an actor, he found he had a talent for design and at seventeen he studied with modernist set designer Norman Bel Geddes for a year and a half. In addition, he was exposed to the work of Joseph Urban, Edward Craig, and Adolph Appia, men who had revolutionized set design and lighting. The lessons in that studio would stay with him for the rest of his life.

Johnson's first set on Broadway was for *Criminal Code,* a drama that he feared would pigeonhole him into doing only black-and-white work. He deliberately set out to get assignments that would be different. Hassard Short recognized his talent and hired him for the striking revue *The Band Wagon,*

which featured a brother-and-sister act from Nebraska by the name of Astaire. The book was directed by George Kaufman, and soon Kaufman and Short hired the now twenty-one-year-old designer to create the settings for *Face the Music*. "I let myself go when I undertook *Face the Music*," he said. "The show gave me a marvelous variety of opportunities, and I had a swell time working out a sequence of problems in lighting, color, and design, which should be as integral a part of the show as the lyrics or music."

OPPOSITE: Johnson's working design for the backdrop for "Franklin D. Roosevelt Inaugurated Tomorrow" in *As Thousands Cheer*.

ABOVE: Johnson used a combination of photographs and primitive drawing to create the look of "World's Wealthiest Man Celebrates 94th Birthday," referencing Rockefeller's ownership of Standard Oil.

The front curtains were his proudest achievement of the show. He believed "they serve as a title page serves a book, and thereafter each set constitutes a chapter." For his next assignment, *As Thousands Cheer*, Johnson turned his penchant for curtains into a leitmotif, projecting newspaper headlines on them to announce each section of the revue. Where once he had gone over the top with a rhinestone-encrusted Venice parodying the revue in *Face the Music*, now he utilized simple flats that he collaged with photos and drawings that bring to mind John Heartfield's Dadaist photomontages.

Johnson eschewed labels, feeling that "whatever is good is always new." He had theoretical ideas about his work, but like Berlin, he "always [had] one eye on the stage door and the other on the box office," he said. "I am not an artist. All I want is to produce a well-balanced show that will be a hit."

After his success on Broadway, Berlin returned to Hollywood in 1934. He would spend the remainder of the decade there creating six films that include some of his greatest screen work. His time was evenly divided between two men: director Mark Sandrich and producer Darryl Zanuck. Each man brought out a different aspect of Berlin's music, for the two could not have been more different. Sandrich, at RKO, was an easygoing young man who nurtured his creative team and understood the needs of the studio. Zanuck, who ran Twentieth Century–Fox, was a brash megalomaniac who fired off memos to intimidate, cajole, and instruct. Despite his abrasive style, Zanuck pulled great performances from actors, directors, and designers.

With Sandrich, Berlin defined the sophisticated musical comedy that he had begun to explore in *Reaching for the Moon*. For Zanuck, Berlin crafted musicals with a distinctly American sensibility. The synthesis of these two strains defined Berlin's films for the rest of his career.

When Astaire wanted to resurrect this dance sequence, seen at right, from a failed Broadway production, Berlin wrote "Top Hat, White Tie, and Tails." The number gave the 1935 film its title, *Top Hat*.

HOLLYWOOD
1934–1942

1934

November 10 *Kid Millions* is released. Eddie Cantor sings "Mandy."

December Berlin starts work on *Top Hat*.

1935

March Berlin moves to the Beverly Wilshire Hotel, where he keeps his piano in a penthouse suite (his bedroom is on the eighth floor).

May The Berlins rent a house in Santa Monica for the summer. Regular guests include Irving Thalberg, Norma Shearer, and the Samuel Goldwyn family.

July First preview of *Top Hat*.

August 29 *Top Hat* opens and work begins on *Follow the Fleet* the following day.

1941

April Berlin, director Mark Sandrich, and Paramount executive Gene Myers meet in San Bernardino to work on *Holiday Inn* script.

August Filming begins on *Holiday Inn*.

December 25 Film of *Louisiana Purchase* is released, starring Bob Hope. Buddy De Sylva produces, but only selected songs of the score are used. The film receives Academy Award nominations for photography and art direction.

December 25 On his radio show Bing Crosby introduces "White Christmas" from the as-yet unreleased *Holiday Inn*.

1942

July 14 *The Pride of the Yankees* is released, featuring "Always."

August 4 *Holiday Inn* premieres.

1936 1937 1938 1939

January 31 One hundred fifty of America's foremost songwriters gather at the Ambassador Hotel in Hollywood to pay tribute to Berlin in honor of his twenty-five years of "leadership in our ranks."

February 20 *Follow the Fleet* is released.

February 12 *On the Avenue* is released.

December 21 Walt Disney's *Snow White and the Seven Dwarfs* is released. Berlin publishes the Oscar-nominated score.

August 3 Nationwide radio tribute to celebrate Berlin's fiftieth birthday and the film *Alexander's Ragtime Band.*

August 19 *Alexander's Ragtime Band* is released.

September 2 *Carefree* is released.

January–May Berlin returns to Hollywood to work on score for *Second Fiddle* and other potential projects with Zanuck.

June 30 *Second Fiddle* is released.

The chorus performs the "Slumming on Park Avenue" number in the revue within the film *On the Avenue.*

LET'S FACE THE MUSIC AND DANCE

"I came here for a two-week visit and decided to do a picture, so signed up with RKO to write the next Fred Astaire and Ginger Rogers movie— which will keep me here til March. It happened to be something I like doing and of course, I made a good contract."

Berlin's postcard to his sister Gussie
from Beverly Hills, December 1935,
shortly before beginning work on *Top Hat*

For his return to Hollywood, Berlin accepted an offer from the small, and sometimes struggling, RKO. The fact that it was not the biggest studio meant he could make a deal that would allow him more creative control over his projects and also a percentage of the film's profits—a first for any songwriter. His previous experience in the movie business had made it clear that, in films as in his other work, he wanted authoritative input on all aspects of the production.

Berlin landed at RKO just as the company found a voice in stylized productions that looked richer than their actual budgets. The "boy wonder" of the studio was twenty-nine-year-old producer Pandro Berman, whose unit was considered the most creative. "Pan" Berman had worked his way through the ranks under David O. Selznick, who had left to work with his father-in-law, Louis B. Mayer, at MGM. Having already been made production chief of all of the studio's films, Berman decided to return to his first love, producing individual pictures. He introduced Berlin to the thirty-three-year-old director Mark Sandrich, who was quickly becoming, in the words of one colleague, "the big shot on the lot."

A rabbi's son from New Brunswick, New Jersey, Sandrich had been studying physics at Columbia when he visited a cousin in Hollywood in 1922. While on a film set he helped a director

Like Berlin, director Mark Sandrich had little formal music education. He felt it gave him the viewpoint of the average viewer.

Rudy Vallee, as movie star Roger Maxwell, films "An Old-Fashioned Tune Is Always New," in *Second Fiddle* (1939).

"I've spent many years in Hollywood," Berlin wrote Ginger Rogers in 1974, "but the most pleasant and memorable ones were those with you and Fred." The trio made three films together between 1935 and 1938. Besides becoming close friends, Berlin and Astaire worked on three more films over the next decade.

stage a gag, and was offered a job. Over the next decade, he became an Oscar-winning director of film shorts, and made the jump to feature films with *Melody Cruise.*

Correspondence between Berlin and Sandrich reveals that they respected and admired each other's abilities. They were both family men who came from religious backgrounds. Both would rather work than go to nightclubs. They assembled a group who would become their professional family for Berlin's three RKO movies. Writers Alan Scott and Dwight Taylor contributed something to each film, and designer Van Nest Polglase and art director Carroll Clark created the "look," which proved to be an important ingredient in the films' success. Of course, the essential elements were Fred Astaire and Ginger Rogers, who had recently been made a starring duo in *The Gay Divorcee.* Today we look at these movies as starring "Astaire and Rogers," or even more intimately "Fred and Ginger," but the creative team looked at them as "Astaire pictures." He was the star, and he created almost all of their dances.

Berlin sat in on most of the story conferences, where the team fashioned ways to integrate the songs and dances into the plot. "We made a definite attempt to have a song and dance forward the story," Sandrich explained after their first film, *Top Hat,* was released. He knew that audiences felt most musical numbers detracted from the story, rather than advancing it, but he recognized that in Astaire he had a performer "who can act, sing, and most importantly, talk with his feet." Citing the start of *Top Hat,* in which Astaire meets Rogers by dancing in the room above hers in their London hotel and then dances the lullaby that puts her to sleep, Sandrich noted that "those routines had narrative value and consequently were worth ten times as much to the picture as just a plain dance would have been."

Sandrich was a meticulous director who, to chart screen time, graphed the script in ten-second increments on index cards, with different colors for different performers. Astaire-Rogers musicals needed four or five dance routines that took up about thirty-five minutes of screen time, each with a story introduction of at least four minutes, "so that they fit logically into whatever story we have time left for," said Sandrich.

They created a sophisticated farce without sex. Sandrich rationalized, "Americans like naughtiness but not smut. In place of heavily risqué lines and action, I substituted that most essential of American interests, good dancing. For misdeeds I substituted misunderstanding." Sandrich went further. "Sex no longer lures the customer. Moviegoers began to yawn about a year ago at heavy love scenes and the surfeited public reaction swept the long-count kiss finale into the discard. Today, the essential quality of a love scene is the playing-down of

ABOVE: Berlin chats on the set with *Top Hat*'s character actors Edward Everett Horton and Helen Broderick.

BELOW: The pantomime dance for "Let's Face the Music and Dance." In the first take, Rogers hit Astaire with the sleeve of her twenty-five-pound dress, leaving him with no memory of his performance. They shot nineteen more takes but went back to the first one for the film.

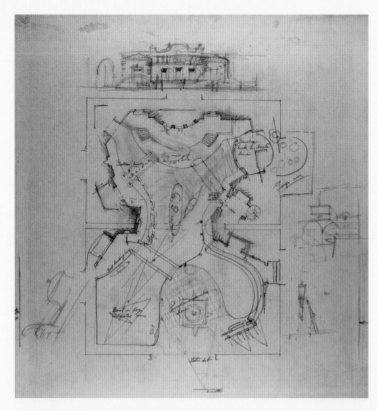

The sleek lines of Carrol Clark's sets for *Top Hat* echo Joseph Urban's work for Ziegfeld. RKO Art Director Van Nest Polglase took a small budget and made it look richer by utilizing geometric patterns on plaster and chrome surfaces to give the flat sets a sense of depth. For the mammoth "Venice" finale, the all-white sets were made whiter by filling the "canal" between two soundstages with black water. The diagram at left shows where each number was to be played. The bridges allowed Astaire and Rogers to make the transition from the intimate balcony setting of "Cheek to Cheek" to the large spaces where he could be "big, bold, and classy" for the closing "Piccolino" number.

OPPOSITE AND BELOW: Two renderings of the Lido set and the actual film set.

When Edward Everett Horton, Astaire's manager in *Top Hat*, suggests he should get married, Astaire responds by singing and dancing "No Strings." This shooting script of the number shows how the fully integrated number was used to introduce Fred to Ginger in the film.

heavy-handed emotion, and the play-up of involved situations that touch the heart and the sense of humor simultaneously." He also had to contend with Joseph Breen's new office of censorship at the Motion Picture Association of America.

In March 1935 it was reported that Berlin had written twenty songs for the film, but in the end, only five were used, with a sixth cut during editing. The score, which included "Cheek to Cheek," "No Strings (I'm Fancy Free)," and "Isn't This a Lovely Day?" is his best complete film work. All of the numbers became standards, and then made history when they simultaneously held five positions on radio's new *Hit Parade.* Four decades later, Berlin would claim that the film's title song, "Top Hat, White Tie, and Tails" was "the best song I wrote for the Astaire films." However, it was "Cheek to Cheek" that was nominated for an Academy Award, though it lost to Harry Warren's "The Lullaby of Broadway" from *The Gold Diggers of 1935. Top Hat,* which was then, and continues to be, the most popular Astaire and Rogers film, was also nominated for best dance direction, best art direction, and best picture (it lost to *Mutiny on the Bounty*).

Berlin and Sandrich's team reassembled for *Follow the Fleet* in August 1935, the day after *Top Hat* was released. "It was high time to take Fred out of tails and put him into a story that would thoroughly Americanize him," said Sandrich in

Astaire and Rogers's relationship is not the primary love story of *Follow the Fleet.* The pair play wisecracking former lovers who soon fall back in love, but Harriet Hilliard, a radio star and soon to be known forever as part of *Ozzie and Harriet,* was the love interest, winning Randolph Scott (below with Fred Astaire) with home cooking and an old ship. Her friends include Lucille Ball (to her right).

December 1935. "Heretofore, he's been sort of a Britisher." To free Astaire from his tuxedo, according to one newspaper column, Berlin suggested filming *Yip, Yip, Yaphank,* which reminded Berman and Sandrich of the sailor play *Shore Leave,* to which the studio owned the rights. Berlin wrote most of the score for *Follow the Fleet* before the script (which he would later tell a friend that he did not like) was finished. One of the film's best numbers had little to do with the script. "Let's Face the Music and Dance" was the first routine in Astaire and Rogers's pictures that they performed completely out of character, playing a staged pantomime to open the number. Over an instrumental introduction, they play a suicidal gambler and a woman contemplating her own death. Astaire's character tries to convince Rogers's character in song not to do it. For audiences, the lyric seemed to reflect the country's idea of the dancing duo during the Depression: "Before they ask us to pay the bill/And while we still have the chance/Let's face the music and dance."

The score is good, but not quite as perfect as that of *Top Hat,* and it was the only one of four Berlin-Sandrich

films not nominated for any Academy Awards. No doubt Berlin's lack of enthusiasm for the script, and the speed with which it was put into production, may have played a role in its shortcomings. Perhaps Berlin's move to his next project at another studio had an effect as well. Soon after his work on *Follow the Fleet* was completed, Berlin began work on *On the Avenue* at Twentieth Century–Fox.

Twentieth Century–Fox was the province of Berlin's oldest friend from the Lower East Side, Joe Schenck, and Schenck's protégé, Darryl Zanuck. Like Berlin, Zanuck, who had little formal education, had a restless ambition to create popular entertainment. His hard-knuckle business acumen was a match for Berlin's, and the two frequently sparred, but always on behalf of the project they were

On the Avenue revolves around a satirical revue of the same name that pokes fun at the wealthy Caraway family. Madeline Carroll (Mimi Caraway) is so upset over Alice Faye's portrayal that she buys the show and closes it, before falling in love with its lead and creator, played by Dick Powell.

working on. With Schenck close by, Berlin never worried too much about Zanuck's incessant memos.

On the Avenue, based on a story that Berlin supplied, is a break from the Berlin-Sandrich collaborations, with only one song integrated into the plot. The rest were performed in the stage revue that was the focus of the film. Berlin saw the film as "a front-page, rather than a back-stage show, with the plot revolving largely about persons in the audience." The plot concerned a satirical revue that pokes fun at a wealthy family. The family is outraged. The daughter (Madeline Carroll) buys the show, closes it, and falls in love with the lead (Dick Powell).

Berlin wanted the numbers performed as they might have been at his own Music Box Theatre. Zanuck agreed, instructing his team to make the numbers look like they could be presented at an ordinary theater, with painted backdrops in colors "that you might see in the *New Yorker* magazine" (though in fact it was a black-and-white film). Instead of competing with "exaggerated [Busby] Berkeley numbers, we want intimacy and smartness." The film shared the same Art Deco sensibility as *Top Hat,* but without the clever variations of the RKO designers.

Berlin saw each of the numbers as "idea songs," which could easily lend themselves to revue staging. As work progressed, he had to make the case to Zanuck not to cut what would become the film's best-known number, "I've Got

The wealthy Caraways, seen in the *On the Avenue* revue. Each revue number was filmed showing the full stage as one would see performances on Broadway.

My Love to Keep Me Warm." The producer felt the picture had more than enough tunes. Berlin realized the score would seem "skimpy," and stressed that he had constructed the song along the same lines as "Cheek to Cheek" and "Let's Face the Music and Dance." Guaranteeing that "I've Got My Love to Keep Me Warm" would be the song that band leaders preferred, he said the song "gives the score body."

The intimate nature of the film was well received, and almost all of the glory was reserved for Berlin's score, which included "This Year's Kisses," "You're Laughing at Me" (a trunk song that Berlin once thought was no good), and "Slumming on Park Avenue." Berlin knew that a score for an Astaire picture was relatively easy to sell to the public and he was proud that his publishing company sold the entire score for the film particularly well.

"A song is only as good as the number of times it is sung," Berlin told a Boston reporter. "And today, instead of singing, people merely listen . . . for music to

live, it must be sung." Berlin had recognized that the sheet-music business was becoming less important, and that for a song to be successful it had to be played on the radio, on records, and in nightclubs. Where once he had written for people to sing his songs, now they listened to them, and both RKO and Zanuck were giving him the best platform for showcasing his wares.

In partnering with Zanuck, who was as yet not known for his musicals (although he had revived the genre in Hollywood with *Forty-Second Street*), Berlin also found a collaborator who shared his enthusiasm for entertainment as an integral part and reflection of America. Zanuck was famous for cobbling together historic cavalcades as backdrops for his films. He sensed that the story of American song could be told through Berlin's music. He had originally wanted to do a screen biopic—a category he had virtually created with films such as *The Mighty Barnum* and *Cardinal Richelieu*—of Berlin. Indeed, when *Alexander's Ragtime Band* was first announced in late 1936, Zanuck wanted the publicity to imply that that was what

The Ritz Brothers play madcap scientists in the revue's opening number, "He Ain't Got Rhythm." Berlin even parodies his recent hit "Cheek to Cheek" when Harry Ritz sings: "Heaven—I see heaven/Through my telescope while gazing/From Mount Wilson's highest peak/I'll explain it all in Latin or in Greek." The chorus adds, "But you're not so hot while dancing cheek to cheek."

the film would be. Berlin, however, was vehemently against dramatizing his life, particularly his private life, so he submitted a story idea that took elements from the four decades of his professional life. Zanuck assigned his favorite writer, Lamar Trotti, to develop the idea, which would eventually be a love triangle set against a gauzy film panorama of the twentieth century, a song-and-dance epic of Berlin's tunes.

Like RKO, Twentieth Century–Fox had a small company of players, writers, and designers to work with. Zanuck took the team of director Henry King and stars Alice Faye, Tyrone Power, and Don Ameche, all of whom had just finished *In Old Chicago,* and added singers Ethel Merman and Jack Haley, and twenty-nine Berlin songs. Berlin wrote three new songs, although one was cut. The score for *Alexander's Ragtime Band* was also the first instance in which Berlin used a mixture of old and new songs in a film. He returned to this format for several other pictures, illustrating the continuing vitality of his catalogue.

OPPOSITE: Ethel Merman first worked with Berlin on *Alexander's Ragtime Band.*

ABOVE: Don Ameche and Alice Faye played lovers in the film.

BELOW: Faye is joined by Jack Haley and Chick Chandler for "The International Rag."

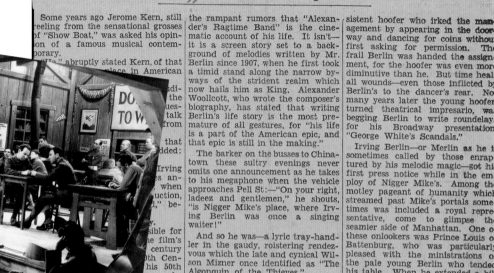

ABOVE: Although Berlin was against using his biography for a film, he did allow elements of it to be used in *Alexander's Ragtime Band*. Here Tyrone Power pulls together an army benefit à la *Yip, Yip, Yaphank*, with the soldiers singing "Oh! How I Hate to Get Up in the Morning."

OPPOSITE: Berlin rehearses with Sophie Tucker, who first sang Berlin songs in vaudeville, for the nationwide radio broadcast celebrating the release of *Alexander's Ragtime Band* and his fiftieth birthday in 1938.

What Zanuck's group lacked was humor. Unlike Sandrich's films, this omnibus was played seriously. While the songs engage a viewer, the melodrama does not, and the story goes on and on. While the reviews were positive, one reviewer at the time wrote, "I don't object to a movie musical's having a hammy plot, but I don't want my nose rubbed in it." Nevertheless, Berlin was nominated for two Oscars, one for "Now It Can Be Told," and the other for best original story. The film had a total of six nominations, including best picture, best art direction, and best editing, but only Alfred Newman won for best music direction.

Less than a month after *Alexander's Ragtime Band* premiered, Berlin's final Astaire-Rogers picture, *Carefree,* was released. A variation on their usual story, the film cast Fred as a psychiatrist, with Ginger as the fiancée of his best friend (Ralph Bellamy), who reluctantly realizes she has fallen for Fred. Sandrich was again at the helm, but his earlier enthusiasm seems to be missing. Rogers refused to show up when production started. She felt that Sandrich was only concerned with Astaire, and was particularly upset when Sandrich told her mother that Ginger, a veteran of nearly forty films, needed to improve her acting and dancing if she wanted to succeed in Hollywood. Sandrich himself was dissatisfied with the studio. After seven years at RKO, this was his final picture for the studio. He left for Paramount before *Carefree* was released in 1938. Berman also jumped ship to MGM.

Berlin must have sensed everyone's dissatisfaction. One witness reported to him that only after Fred and Ginger recorded three songs was "the old spirit . . . back."

The finished score is only five songs. Four more songs were composed but did not make the final cut. Among the five, only three are sung, since two are played as instrumentals with Astaire performing a golf routine to "Since They Turned Loch Lomond into Swing." There are two classic songs, the great "Change Partners," a song with no regular chorus, only the title slipping in and out of the lines, and the innovative "I Used to Be Color Blind." With the song's Oscar nomination in 1940, Berlin competed against his own "Now It Can Be Told" for best song. The Academy Award went instead to "Over the Rainbow" from *The Wizard of Oz*.

For Berlin's next picture with Zanuck, the songwriter suggested another compilation of works centered "around the singers of popular songs . . . Nora Bayes, Al Jolson, [and] Belle Baker" in a film appropriately to be titled *Tin Pan Alley.* Zanuck stroked the songwriter's ego by suggesting it would be much better as *Irving Berlin's Tin Pan Alley* but put off announcing it until the day after *Alexander's Ragtime Band* opened in New York. But by then,

Elizabeth was born June 16, 1936, and completed the Berlin family. The Scottish nanny hired to take care of Linda was now shifted to her care, and the Berlin family resumed its familiar pace. With Irving firmly established in Hollywood, there was talk of moving out West. But both Ellin and Irving felt it was important for the girls to be raised in New York, so Ellin (at first with Elizabeth) commuted between Hollywood and Manhattan, and the whole family spent summers and holidays together. When Elizabeth was two, her father bought a country home in the Catskills, where the family would spend many happy times together.

Elizabeth contributed to Berlin's biggest Broadway hit. It was in her schoolbooks that Berlin found the names of various Indian tribes for "I'm an Indian Too" in *Annie Get Your Gun*.

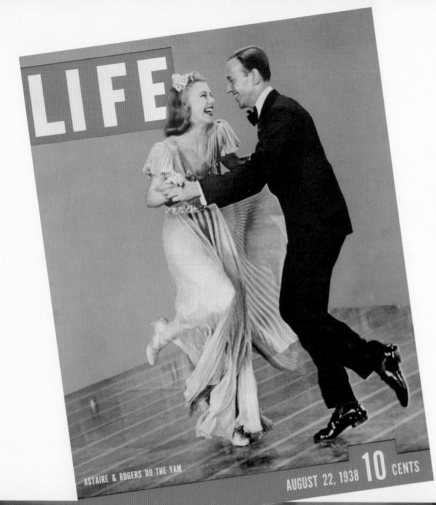

ABOVE: The combination of Astaire, Rogers, and Berlin was headline news. The week that *Carefree* was released it was such a big story that it made the cover of *Life*, as well as other publications across the country.

LEFT: After Astaire (dancing with Louella Gear) realizes he is in love with Rogers, he tries to break into her dance with fiancée Ralph Bellamy by singing "Won't you change partners and dance with me?"

OPPOSITE: Astaire and Rogers dance in a dream sequence in *Carefree*'s "I Used to Be Color Blind."

Berlin's films mirrored the mood of America. In 1935's *Top Hat*, the ultramodern set design allowed audiences to escape from their everyday lives. By 1938's *Carefree*, Americans across the country were exploring their rustic roots. Grant Wood and Thomas Hart Benton celebrated this diversity in their paintings, and RKO's set designers touched their American heritage by creating a neocolonial look for Ginger Rogers's home in the film. *Carefree* introduced a more American look to film musicals, presaging the simplified look of *Holiday Inn*. This "Early American" decoration was soon copied by homeowners.

TOP: Ginger Rogers's bedroom in *Top Hat*.
BOTTOM: Rogers's living room in *Carefree*.

Berlin had cooled on the idea. By October 27, 1938, he wrote Zanuck suggesting a film commenting on current events, but not as propaganda. "Maybe an angle on 'peace' and 'democracy.'" Glued to the radio that summer for news of the worsening conditions in Europe made him want to write a song that would express his feeling of gratitude for what America represented. Less than three weeks later, Kate Smith would introduce "God Bless America" on her radio show. All fall Berlin had been in New York as his father-in-law lay dying. In his correspondence with Zanuck, Zanuck suggested a picture with the ice-skating star Sonja Henie. Berlin was interested if he could contribute more than just a score, feeling that another Henie movie was "as old a story as just another Astaire-Rogers picture." For the next month the two squabbled in their letters about the value of doing another film featuring old songs, before finally settling on a picture for the ice skater.

Second Fiddle was a gentle satire on the long search for the Scarlett role in David O. Selznick's *Gone with the Wind*, a touch of *Cyrano de Bergerac*, and the bogus romance cooked up by press agents between Tyrone Power and Sonja Henie when they

became stars. In the movie they do fall in love, except that Power is the press agent who concocts the romance between Henie's character and Rudy Vallee's. In the end, Berlin felt *Second Fiddle* was a compromise with Zanuck. Berlin contributed four songs he had intended for an aborted *Music Box Revue,* including "The Song of the Metronome" and "I'm Sorry for Myself." In January and February of 1939 he composed two more songs for the film, including "I Poured My Heart into a Song," which was nominated for the best-song Oscar. Nevertheless, the score is the least memorable of all his screen efforts. Though Berlin and Zanuck talked about a screen biopic of the Music Box Theatre called *Say It with Music,* they could never agree on terms or performers.

Berlin spent the fall of 1939 working on the score of the Broadway musical comedy *Louisiana Purchase,* which opened in May 1940. In the meantime, he had drafted an outline for a stage revue based on holidays throughout the year. He

ABOVE: Rudy Vallee sings the Oscar nominated "I Poured My Heart into a Song" to Sonja Henie. Henie's character thinks he has written it for her, but it turns out to be Tyrone Power's words and feelings about her.

OPPOSITE: Berlin returned to his roots by writing a novelty dance song, "Back to Back," for *Second Fiddle.* Here Edna May Oliver, Tyrone Power, Sonja Henie, and Rudy Vallee follow the song's instructions.

ABOVE: Berlin outlined his idea for a stage revue based on holidays celebrated throughout the year. He developed the idea into a film with Mark Sandrich. They set it at a Connecticut inn that is only open on fifteen holidays a year. The film inspired the name of the Holiday Inn hotel chain.

OPPOSITE, TOP: Astaire and Marjorie Reynolds dance to the Washington's Birthday number, "I Can't Tell a Lie."

OPPOSITE, BOTTOM: To hide his girl from his partner, Bing Crosby's character, Jim Hardy, dons blackface for the Lincoln's Birthday song "Abraham," one of the last blackface performances on screen. When African Americans objected to the use of the word *darky* in the song, Berlin apologized and changed the word to *negro* in all future sheet music.

saw Sandrich in Washington and shared it with him and they knew they had the makings of a good film. After two lackluster movie experiences, Berlin was anxious to create another great picture with Sandrich like *Top Hat*.

With Sandrich now producing and directing at Paramount, they had a different group to work with. Bing Crosby, perhaps America's most popular entertainer, was the star of the studio. They had hoped to get Alan Scott—"one of the family," according to Berlin—to write the script but eventually playwright Elmer Rice was hired. Berlin's letters and telegrams to Sandrich betray an excitement missing from his voluminous correspondence with Zanuck.

Astaire's signing on as Crosby's partner sealed the reunion. Berlin and Sandrich had hoped to get Mary Martin, but she became pregnant and dropped out. They considered Ginger Rogers, but the budget forced them to hire an unknown dancer, Marjorie Reynolds, whose voice had to be dubbed. The movie was titled *Holiday Inn,* and the score came quickly. There were eleven new tunes in all—the sum of his previous two film scores—as well as two older songs, "Lazy" and "Easter Parade."

Berlin believed that his Valentine song, "Be Careful, It's My Heart" would be the big hit. But audiences in the first fall of World War II favored "White Christmas." The song would become the most popular song and most widely recorded song of all time, and it would finally win an Oscar for the songwriter.

The summer of 1942, with the film completed, both Sandrich and Berlin were anxious to aid the country as it entered the war. In June, Sandrich organized the Hollywood Victory Caravan, which gathered a host of movie stars in a production that made a three-week cross-country tour and netted $730,000 for the Army and Navy Relief Funds. Berlin was already rehearsing *This Is the Army,* which would open on July 4. When *Holiday Inn* opened in August 1942, Sandrich explained that the film was a "complete picture of America and its people, seen through its holidays, with music carrying out the commemorative spirit of democracy, which glories not in anniversaries of famous battles but in such human celebrations as our Fourth of July, great Americans such as Lincoln, [and] the religious joy of Christmas." Berlin and Sandrich saw it as "Americana," not propaganda. They had wanted to make an entertaining movie, "but subconsciously I must have realized its purely American—and hence patriotic—implications," said Sandrich a week later. Filming was complete before Pearl Harbor, but the simplicity of the production seemed to anticipate wartime austerity.

When the film opened, Berlin was receiving standing ovations every night in a production that did not deal with "patriotic implications" in the abstract. Its message blared from its title: *This Is the Army.*

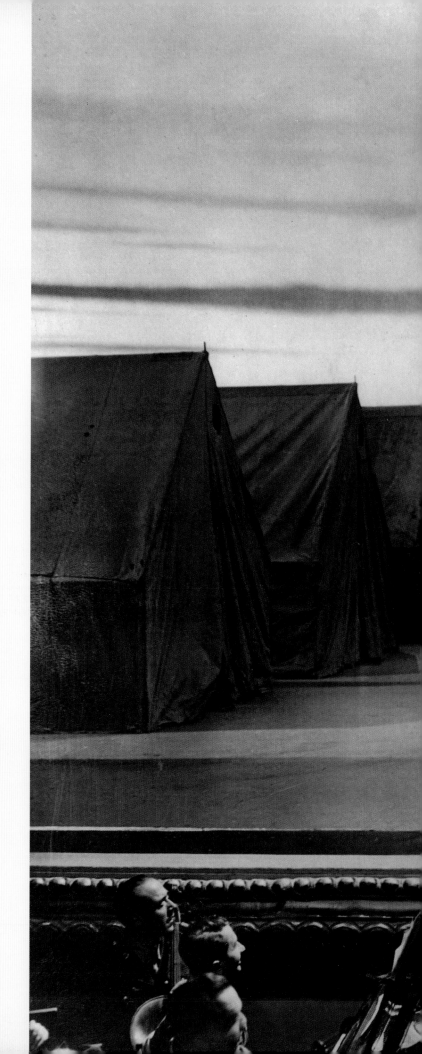

In 1925 Jerome Kern famously declared that "Irving Berlin has no place in American music. Irving Berlin *is* American music." Kern recognized that Berlin had captured the American vernacular in both melody and lyric from the very beginning of his career. Berlin was grateful for the opportunities that America had afforded him; he was glad to write patriotic songs when he felt the country needed them as he did in World War I. But he never wanted to exploit his patriotism.

"A patriotic song has got to be good, or it's unworthy of publication," Berlin said in 1940. "It can be simply a trick—an applause trap, like waving a flag at the end of the third act, which just about forces an audience to clap. There is nothing wrong in doing it, as long as it isn't just a device. If the song or the performance deserves applause, that's all right, but patriotism can be the refuge of a scoundrel in the entertainment world as in other spheres."

By 1938 he was eager to express his gratitude to the nation, and for the next five years his efforts put a song in his countrymen's hearts, with a show for them to applaud, and millions of dollars into the coffers of worthy causes. All without earning a penny for himself.

Berlin sings "Oh! How I Hate to Get Up in the Morning" in the film version of *This Is the Army*.

AMERICA
1938-1945

"God Bless America" and *This Is the Army*

1938

September 30 Berlin returns from *Alexander's Ragtime Band* promotional tour in England and attempts to write a "peace" song.

November 10 Kate Smith introduces "God Bless America" on her weekly radio broadcast.

1940

June Berlin receives honorary doctorate from Bucknell University. In appreciation he endows a music scholarship in the name of his friend and lawyer Francis Gilbert.

1942

March 11 War Department writes to ask for a revival of *Yip, Yip, Yaphank.* More than a month later he arrives at Camp Upton on Long Island and writes a new show called *This Is the Army.*

July 4 *This Is the Army* opens on Broadway. The show runs until September 26. National tour starts in Washington, D.C.

November 7 Berlin is a pallbearer at George M. Cohan's funeral at St. Patrick's Cathedral.

1943

July 29 The film of *This Is the Army* premieres. Ray Heindorf wins an Oscar for his musical scoring.

November *This Is the Army* opens in London and tours the United Kingdom through January.

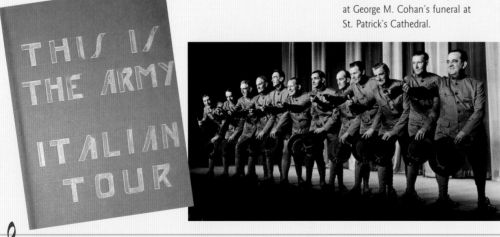

1944

April 3 *This Is the Army* opens in Italy and tours through July.

1945

September Berlin returns to America and ends his partnership with Saul Bornstein. He establishes the Irving Berlin Music Company.

January Berlin rejoins the company of *This Is the Army* in New Guinea and tours the South Pacific through March.

October Berlin is awarded the Medal of Merit by President Harry S. Truman.

The finale of *This Is the Army*.

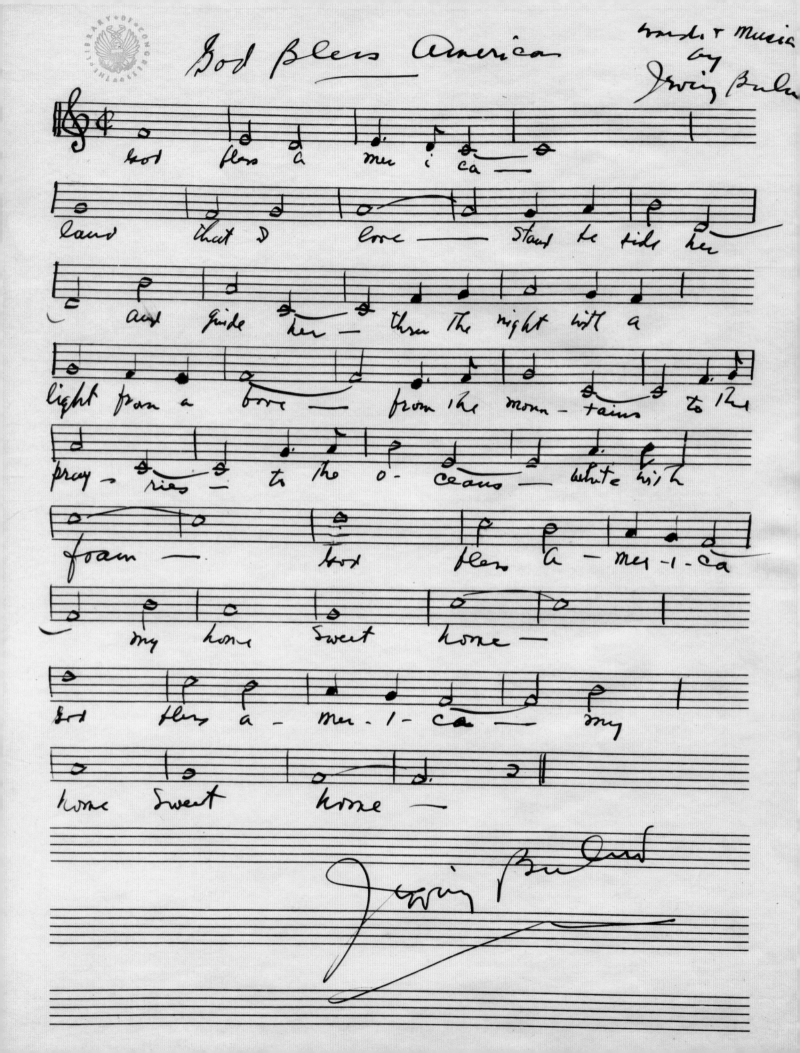

WHAT'S WRONG WITH A PATRIOTIC SONG?

"I have one bit of news that I think will interest you," Berlin wrote his friend, songwriter Harry Ruby, in a telegram on November 9, 1938. "Do you remember a song I wrote during the war that you always liked, called 'God Bless America'? Well, Kate Smith asked me for a song to do at the end of her program on Armistice Day and I put a verse to it and rewrote the chorus and she will sing it tomorrow night. I am wiring you today to listen in, if you can. I have no idea what I will do with this song after her broadcast but I like the chorus very much."

The previous summer, Berlin, like many Americans, was concerned about the growing threat of war in Europe. He wanted to write a song that would express his feelings of how fortunate he was to live in America. After a promotional tour in England for *Alexander's Ragtime Band,* which coincided with Neville Chamberlain's visit to Hitler and the signing of the Munich Pact, he tried to write a song. Fifteen years later he wrote to Abel Green of *Variety,* "I remember finishing a chorus of a song called 'Thanks America,' which I tore up because it was very bad. It seemed like a bad editorial set to music."

Berlin then remembered a song he had rejected for *Yip, Yip, Yaphank* where Ruby had served as his musical secretary, a march that he felt was "painting the lily" at the conclusion of the patriotic show. He revised the words, changing "to the right with a light from above" to "through the night with a light from above . . ." because in the intervening twenty years "to the right" had taken on a political significance he felt was wrong for the song. Other lyric changes altered the march to a simpler but more majestic melody.

Berlin was happy to provide his "new" song, "God Bless America," to Kate Smith's manager for her November 10 broadcast, and he made certain it got to the printers so the sheet music could be published simultaneously. A day before its debut, he received the first sheet music proofs, and he decided to tinker a bit more with the melody to get it just

"God Bless America" was the rare song that Berlin copied out in his own hand.

The performer most closely associated with the song "God Bless America" is Kate Smith. In the 1970s, Smith's career was revived when the Philadelphia Flyers hockey team began playing her recording of the song at the start of their home games, and she often performed live at championship games. Smith and her rendition have since been immortalized in this larger-than-life sculpture by Mark Mellon, which stands in front of the Flyers' home arena.

right. He recognized that it was a special song, one that could articulate the emotion he felt for his country. In 1967 he would say that " 'God Bless America' is closer to me than any song I have ever written." If Berlin's career is seen as the fulfillment of the American Dream, this song is its anthem.

Harry Ruby wrote Berlin three days after the broadcast, "I think it is a swell song and I know of nothing better to aid in whipping up Pro-American sentiment. The song had the right quality and might carry on way beyond your expectations." Whatever Berlin's expectations were, he could never have imagined the groundswell of its popularity. Smith continued to sing it every week on her radio show— Berlin felt that "Smith is not [only the] first, but she remains the best" interpreter of the song. The public embraced it and articles praising it appeared in almost every type of publication. The title alone became a phrase to express one's patriotism. Some critics worried that the separation of church and state was violated by the song, and other, more antisemitic, voices wondered whether this immigrant Jewish songwriter should be linking God and America to make money. But their voices were drowned out by the overwhelmingly positive response to the song.

OPPOSITE: Berlin watches a rehearsal of *This Is the Army* at the Broadway Theatre, 1942.

BELOW: With Berlin watching, Kate Smith writes a check to the Army Emergency Relief Fund during the run of *This Is the Army*.

OVERLEAF: Berlin watches rehearsals of *This Is the Army* at Camp Upton in the spring of 1942.

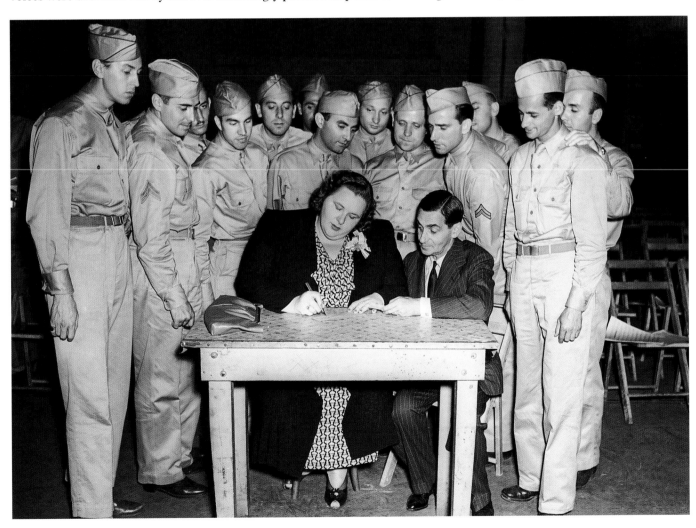

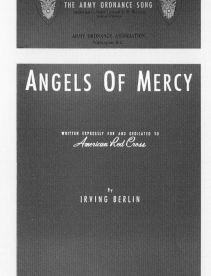

As World War II approached, Berlin was happy to write songs for various government agencies either to promote awareness, boost morale, or raise funds, but he went to extraordinary lengths to ensure that all the monies generated in such efforts went to their specific causes. All were strictly noncommercial for Berlin, and he made no profit from any of these songs or *This Is the Army*. For the show, he set up a separate publishing company to take care of all its business. Combined with the proceeds from "God Bless America," Berlin raised more than $20 million for the government and charity through his work.

"The Star-Spangled Banner" had only been adopted as the official national anthem in 1931, but some, including Eleanor Roosevelt, thought that the anthem should be easier to sing. There were efforts to make "God Bless America" the new national anthem, but Berlin was opposed to the idea. "A national anthem is something that develops naturally through age, tradition, historic significance, and general recognition," Berlin stated. "You can't legislate one. They arise alone and stand the test of time. We've got a good national anthem; you can't have two."

Soon after Kate Smith's broadcast, he decided to give the instantly valuable copyright to charity. He spent six months trying to donate it to his first choice, the Red Cross, but chairman Norman Davis suggested "that the [Boy] Scouts may be more readily identified in the minds of the public as a more colorful organization and a distinctly patriotic movement." Berlin agreed, and established the God Bless America Fund, an independent trust that turned over the song's steady revenue— by this time now over ten million dollars—to the Boy and Girl Scouts.

Berlin felt fortunate that he had not used the song in 1918, when it would have been "just another war song." What he wanted most at this time was a "peace" song. In effect he wrote a folk song, one that has been sung by generations of children and adults, many of whom have no idea that Berlin wrote it, or that it was written relatively recently. It has become part of the American landscape. To people like Woody Guthrie, Berlin's idea was reactionary. After hearing the song over and over again in the summer of 1939, Guthrie was inspired to write his folk classic "This Land Is Your Land," originally titled "God Blessed America."

ABOVE: Berlin, alone on his cot, at the beginning of "Oh! How I Hate to Get Up in the Morning" in *This Is the Army*.

LEFT: Berlin puts the chorus line through its paces. Left to right: director Ezra Stone, Berlin, stage manager Alan Anderson, choreographer Robert Sidney (kneeling), and dancers.

Berlin revived the minstrel number "Mandy" for *This Is the Army,* featuring (below) Richard Irving and Fred Kelly (Gene's brother).

Yet Berlin's patriotism was no last refuge. He understood the power of a song to lift a singer's heart. After nearly a decade of global economic depression and strife, Berlin made an active response to the fears and concerns Americans had about the world.

As the war approached, Berlin wrote "Any Bonds Today?" and "I Paid My Income Tax Today" for the Treasury Department; "Arms for the Love of America" for the Army Ordnance Department; "Angels of Mercy" for the Red Cross; and others for the navy (at Walter Winchell's request), youth organizations, and the infantile paralysis fund, as well as songs denouncing Hitler.

Like many Americans, after Pearl Harbor the songwriter wanted to help. Too old to enlist, he was thinking about reviving *Yip, Yip, Yaphank,* and in March 1942 the War Department wrote to ask for exactly that as a morale-booster and fundraiser. A month later he was back at Camp Upton, only to realize that the title and mood of the show was wrong for this conflict. In World War I, he came to Camp Upton as a young man near the end of the war. In World War II, he had come to the camp as a fifty-four-year-old man at the war's start. In a month he wrote more than ten new songs, and the effort bore the title *This Is the Army.* Berlin started to assemble a cast of performers from the ranks of the entire army,

including African-American performers, making his company the first integrated unit in the history of the armed forces. Although he still used blackface in the show, Berlin was sensitive toward racial discrimination. Throughout the show's Broadway run, national tour, and international tour, the company accepted no invitations unless the entire company was included.

Radio star Sergeant Ezra Stone directed the show and the three-hundred-soldier cast included other Broadway veterans. Berlin chose the revue format to celebrate the soldiers who fight for freedom around the world, as Berlin wrote:

> This time we will make certain
> That this time is the last time;
> This time we will not say "Curtain"
> Till we ring it down in their own hometown.
> For this time
> We are out to finish
> The job we started then,
> Clean it up for all time this time,
> So we don't have to do it again.

James Cross sings, "An olive drab color scheme—that's what the well-dressed man in Harlem will wear," against a simple but striking set. Below: filming the same number in Hollywood.

Like its predecessor, *This Is the Army* got laughs from cross-dressing soldiers in the female roles. Imagine a young Burl Ives dressed in a German Fräulein's outfit, and you might get some idea of the humor. As in vaudeville, jugglers, acrobats, and a unicyclist were sprinkled through the numbers. During the Broadway run and national tour, members of the old troupe of *Yip, Yip, Yaphank* joined Berlin onstage in their doughboy outfits before he sang "Oh! How I Hate to Get Up in the Morning." Berlin would continue with the show, with only short breaks, for the next two and one-half years.

The original Yankee Doodle Dandy, George M. Cohan, must have approved of the show, which opened in 1942, on the last Fourth of July of his life. Berlin was upholding a tradition, and it was a hit to boot. Al Hirschfeld reported to friends in California that "they're standing 'em three deep to see the show." As he had with "God Bless America," Berlin articulated people's feeling for the country with the right mixture of humility, and now, bravado and humor. To Gilbert Seldes, he

OPPOSITE, TOP: Berlin and Ezra Stone. Stone was a radio and stage veteran who directed the show.

OPPOSITE, BOTTOM: Berlin sings "Alexander's Ragtime Band" to troops aboard the USS *Arkansas* on July 25, 1944.

ABOVE: The company on the Warner Brothers lot to make the film. Publicists were warned not to glamorize the soldiers so that other soldiers' parents would not think company members had it easy.

LEFT: "The show has become a symbol of what they like about Americans," Irving wrote to Ellin from London. Referring to a new song, "['My British Buddy'] is quite popular now and you can hear them singing it on the streets." Here the song is filmed for the movie's English release.

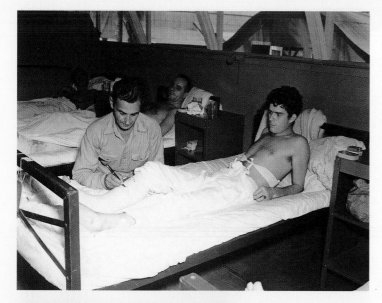

Irving Berlin was composer, performer, and producer of
This Is the Army. A civilian, he was in charge of more
than three hundred soldiers. When not on stage or
reworking the show for different venues, Berlin visited
army hospitals, sang for the troops, and took names and
addresses to write to family members once he got home.
"Mr. B," as he was known to all in his company of soldiers, was also one of the "boys." The soldiers understood
that Berlin was giving his all with his more-than-two-year
commitment to the production and tour.

Berlin prepares to go onstage while on tour.

wrote, "I very consciously kept away from flag-waving to the extent that I didn't even use 'God Bless America,' which seemed to be a 'must,' in view of the fact that it was originally written for *Yip, Yip, Yaphank*." As with "God Bless America," he donated all of his profits as composer, lyricist, and publisher, this time to the Army Emergency Relief Fund.

When *This Is the Army* opened, Berlin's "The Girl on the Police Gazette" could be heard in Mike Todd's *Star and Garter,* while Gypsy Rose Lee performed. Less than one month later, *Holiday Inn* opened in theaters across the country. "White Christmas" broke out of that film as a wartime anthem of a different sort, selling thousands of copies of both sheet music and records. It appealed to soldiers who longed to be home, and their loved ones who looked forward to a return to the simple pleasures of a holiday celebrated together. Berlin wrote Sandrich, "The song seems to have a quality that can be applied to the world situation as it exists today.

The "Ladies of the Chorus" number at the Rome Opera House in 1944. Originally written for *Yip, Yip, Yaphank*, it proved just as popular in *This Is the Army*.

I understand many copies are being sent to the boys overseas, and it is just possible, while it isn't a war song, it can be easily associated with it." The song caught national sentiment and helped to nationalize, and to an extent even secularize, the holiday. If he did not get to write the national anthem, he certainly had the signature song for the national holiday. Its universal appeal made him realize that the song belonged in a special category. "There are only so many of these kinds of songs in a songwriter's system," he wrote to Sandrich. "They are the milestones, all the others are 'filler-ins,' even if they become popular."

Berlin spent the next six months on the road with the company of *This Is the Army*, performing every night, and taking care of business during the day. It was soon clear that a movie version would be made and Berlin hoped to work with

We joined the army, but look at us now.
We're the ladies of the chorus,
Dolled up as girls to our ears,
With cute golden tresses,
In corsets and dresses,
But don't get any strange ideas.
From "Ladies of the Chorus"

When the film of *This Is the Army* was made, publicists were advised not to allow photographs of any of the soldiers in drag. But like its predecessor, the show got many laughs from cross-dressing soldiers in the female roles. Berlin drew on the traditions of minstrel shows, drag, vaudeville, and revue to craft an all-American show. Clockwise from top right: the Dream Ballet; Carl Van Vechten portraits of Nelson Barcliff in and out of costume; Berlin chats up a soldier backstage.

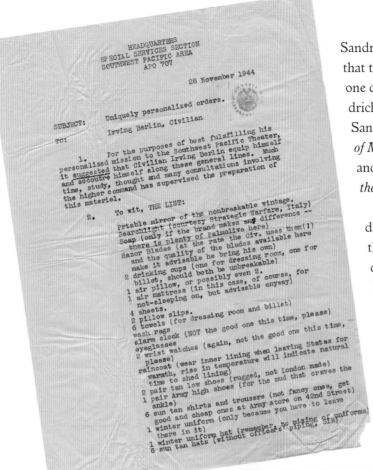

HEADQUARTERS
SPECIAL SERVICES SECTION
SOUTHWEST PACIFIC AREA
APO 707

28 November 1944

SUBJECT: Uniquely personalized orders.

TO: Irving Berlin, Civilian

1.   For the purposes of best fulsfilling his
personalized mission to the Southwest Pacific Theater,
it suggested that Civilian Irving Berlin equip himself
and accoutre himself along these general lines. Much
time, study, thought and many consultations involving
the higher command has supervised the preparation of
this materiel.

2.   To wit, THE LIST:

Prtable mirror of the nonbreakable vintage.
Searchlight (courtesy Strategic Warfare, Italy)
Soap (only if the brand makes any difference --
     there is plenty of Palmolive here)
Razor Blades (at the rate the Civ. uses them(I)
     and the quality of the blades available here
     make it advisable he bring his own)
2 drinking cups (one for dressing room, one for
     billet, should both be unbreakable)
1 air pillow, or possibly even 2.
1 air mattress (in this case, of course, for
     not-sleeping on, but advisable anyway)
4 sheets.
2 pillow slips.
6 towels (for dressing room and billet)
wash rags
alarm clock (NOT the good one this time, please)
eyeglasses (again, not the good one this time,
     please)
2 wrist watches
raincoat (wear inner lining when leaving States for
     warmth, rise in temperature will indicate natural
     time to shed lining)
2 pair tan low shoes (rugged, not London made)
1 pair Army high shoes (for the mud that craves the
     ankle)
6 sun tan shirts and trousers (not fancy ones, get
     good and cheap ones at Army store on 42nd Street)
1 winter uniform (only because you have to leave
     there in it)
1 winter uniform hat (remember, no mixing of uniforms,
6 sun tan hats (without officers' piping, SIR)

Berlin returned to the states in the fall of 1944. Before he joined *This Is the Army* in the South Pacific, his publicist and right-hand man Ben Washer advised what supplies to bring (above). Even when he was not on tour with *This Is the Army* Berlin entertained troops (right).

Sandrich. The two started to plan the production and agreed that the entire venture should be noncommercial, with everyone donating their services. When Warner Bros. outbid Sandrich's Paramount, they were both deeply disappointed. Sandrich went on to make a film about nurses called *Angels of Mercy,* and the two planned on making another Crosby and Astaire picture as soon as Berlin was done with *This Is the Army.*

Michael Curtiz, who also directed *Mammy,* ended up directing the film version. He and Berlin realized that there was no way to capture on film the excitement that a company of three hundred could summon every night. Instead, the film version of *This Is the Army* is more or less a hagiography of the show, with the lightly fictionalized origins of "God Bless America" thrown in for good measure. A love story between Ronald Reagan and Joan Leslie is the pivot of the plot. Kate Smith re-created her original broadcast of "God Bless America," even approximating her same spoken introduction. The reverence for the story of the song and show is touching. Berlin's performance of

his World War I song is immortalized in this Technicolor production.

After filming in Hollywood, the company, minus the Hollywood stars, went on to tour the United Kingdom, Italy, the Middle East (without Berlin), the South Pacific, and eventually, the Philippines. It is doubtful that Berlin's friends thought he would stay on for the whole tour, but he felt he owed it to "the boys," the show, and his country, so at the height of his powers he channeled his energy into the effort. He wrote special songs for the different locales, but during the day visited hospitals, gave impromptu performances for soldiers, and dealt with changing elements of the show, which was constantly being revised to accommodate the venue.

By the time the show reached the South Pacific, Berlin had taken to singing "God Bless America" in addition to "Oh! How I Hate to Get Up in the Morning," which he realized made a better finale for his performance. The audiences of soldiers, and locals who saw the American forces as liberators, evidently shared the sentiment. Before singing the number, he asked the audience to light their lighters or matches. "We first black out and the effect is thrilling," he wrote his wife. "Very much like looking down on Hollywood at night from a mountain top (God forbid). But to see an audience of 11,000 light up like so many flickering stars would even impress Hassard Short."

By the time he got to the Philippines, the fifty-seven-year-old Berlin was exhausted, but the tour's goodwill renewed him. A group of children singing their own Filipino-specific words to "God Bless America" inspired him to write one for the Filipinos, "Heaven Watch the Philippines," again to benefit their Girl and Boy Scouts. The company, along with one hundred school children, presented it on opening night. He wrote Ellin right after the show, "All the boys felt this was the biggest moment in our show since the opening in New York. I think so too. London and the other high spots were glamorous, but tonight's finale was equally moving as Kate Smith's introduction of 'God Bless America.' I wish you could have seen it."

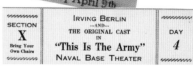

He soon would return to his family and his business, but the idea of what it meant to be American stayed with him. All of his remaining Broadway shows were about Americana. His films viewed show business as a mirror of American progress. But it was "God Bless America" and *This Is the Army* that had allowed him to express his gratitude to the "land that I love."

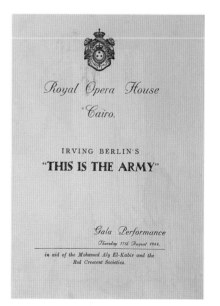

To hear Irving Berlin's Broadway work in the 1940s, one had only to go to the Imperial Theatre on West Forty-fifth Street. Three of his shows, *Louisiana Purchase, Annie Get Your Gun,* and *Miss Liberty*, spent half the decade at that theater. All three are "situation shows," as Berlin referred to musicals with integrated librettos and music, and all draw on American history and politics. Berlin understood Broadway's move from urban sophistication to American folklore, signaled by the success of Rodgers and Hammerstein's *Oklahoma!* in 1943. Even his films of this period had distinctly American settings and themes. For the rest of his active career, Berlin remained interested in mining aspects of Americana for his Broadway work. With the integrated numbers in *Annie Get Your Gun,* Berlin wrote no fewer than eight hits, his best Broadway score. Berlin took the traits of the show's characters and, as he did with all his songs, found new "angles" on universal themes. When someone remarked that the show seemed old-fashioned, Berlin replied, "Yes, an old-fashioned smash."

The cast of *Louisiana Purchase* takes a curtain call, 1940.

BROADWAY
1940-1949

1940

1941

1942

1945

May 28 Berlin ends his more than five-year Hollywood sojourn when *Louisiana Purchase* opens at the Imperial Theatre.

June 14 After 444 performances, *Louisiana Purchase* closes on Broadway and then goes on tour for another year.

July 4 *This Is the Army* opens at the Broadway Theatre, running until September 26. A national tour follows, as well as a film of the show, before it leaves for England, Italy, and the South Pacific. Berlin will spend nearly three years with the production.

November 11 Jerome Kern dies. Within a month, producers Rodgers and Hammerstein ask Berlin to take over for Kern on a new musical, then titled *Annie Oakley*.

1946

1949

1950

May 16 *Annie Get Your Gun*, starring Ethel Merman, opens at the Imperial Theatre.

January Berlin finishes the score for *Miss Liberty*.

February 12 *Annie Get Your Gun* closes after 1,157 performances. It is Merman's (and Berlin's) longest run on Broadway.

May 13 Rehearsals begin for *Miss Liberty*.

July 15 *Miss Liberty* opens at the Imperial.

April 8 After 308 performances, *Miss Liberty* closes and starts a national tour.

On a visit to Mexico in 1948, the Berlins were introduced to Diego Rivera, who wanted to paint the songwriter's portrait. Berlin demurred but later commissioned the artist to paint a cover for a new song he had written, "I Gave Her My Heart in Acapulco." This painting was never used, as it was deemed "too cartoonish" and with its scenes of interracial couples frolicking in the water too advanced for the South, where sheet music still sold well.

ANYTHING YOU CAN DO, I CAN DO BETTER

When Berlin returned to New York from Hollywood after his unsatisfactory experience with *Second Fiddle* in 1939, he was determined to stay and work on Broadway. He continued to supply popular songs to his publishing company, but he husbanded much of his creative output for films and stage at this point in his career. He wanted to stage another *Music Box Revue,* and even composed songs for the production, but it never materialized. Berlin knew how important casting was on a revue, and without the "right people" it was not worth doing.

When his lawyer, Abe Berman, who worked as both an attorney and an agent for a number of Broadway figures, suggested that Berlin collaborate with another client, producer Buddy DeSylva, on a new show, the songwriter was intrigued. DeSylva was himself a prolific songwriter who worked often with composer Ray Henderson and lyricist Lew Brown, penning such classics as "Button Up Your Overcoat," "Look for the Silver Lining," and "California, Here I Come." He had also collaborated with Jerome Kern on "Look for the Silver Lining" and George Gershwin on "Somebody Loves Me." DeSylva had been in Hollywood during the same years as Berlin, working as a songwriter and producer. That fall he was preparing to produce Cole Porter's musical comedy *DuBarry Was a Lady,* starring Ethel Merman, Bert Lahr, and Betty Grable, for which he had also written the book. The show opened and was a hit in December 1939.

DeSylva was eager to work with Berlin and shared his idea of a musical satire based on corrupt Southern politicians like Huey Long. They hired George Kaufman's writing partner on *Of Thee I Sing*, Morrie Ryskind, to write the book for the new show. Since Long's story ended in his assassination, Ryskind concocted a more genial story of a bumbling Republican senator who comes to New Orleans to investigate corruption, and the attempts by the local politicians to put him in compromising positions so they can blackmail him into leaving them alone. Early on it was decided to call the show *Louisiana Purchase.*

A composite of scenes from 1949's *Miss Liberty.*

Al Hirschfeld visited Morrie Ryskind, Victor Moore, and George Balanchine at a rehearsal of *Louisiana Purchase* in April 1940.

They signed William Gaxton and Victor Moore, who had first teamed together in *Of Thee I Sing* in 1932, and were enjoying success as the leads in Cole Porter's *Leave It to Me,* which closed that fall. Before Ryskind had even started the script, Berlin and DeSylva approached Marlene Dietrich for a part as an exotic temptress who would put the investigating senator at risk. When she wasn't available, they considered the singer Hildegard before settling on Vera Zorina, a beautiful ballerina who was the wife of George Balanchine. She had caused a sensation in her debut the year before in Rodgers and Hart's *I Married an Angel,* as the heavenly creature of the title. Balanchine had choreographed that show, and would stage her numbers in *Louisiana Purchase.*

ABOVE: George Balanchine choreographed the ballets in *Louisiana Purchase* that featured his wife, Vera Zorina (shown here with Charles Laskey). Carl Randall staged the other dances.

BOTTOM AND OPPOSITE: Irene Bordoni kept a scrapbook of hand-colored photographs from her run in *Louisiana Purchase.* Left to right: Bordoni, Victor Moore, and Vera Zorina.

Berlin worked quickly, writing many of the songs in the first few months of 1940. He took one song, "Sex Marches On," from his aborted *Music Box Revue* and "It's a Lovely Day Tomorrow," which he had originally written in December 1939 as a morale booster for the English, who were at a low point in World War II. With minor lyric revisions, it proved to be a poignant song of hope sung in the

A contact sheet featuring all the principals in various costumes by Tom Lee: William Gaxton, Victor Moore, Vera Zorina, Carol Bruce, and Irene Bordoni.

show by long-time theater star Irene Bordoni. Vera Lynn's recording made it a wartime anthem. The score also included such future classics as "What Chance Have I with Love" and "Fools Fall in Love."

Louisiana Purchase opened in May 1940 and turned out to be one of the big hits of the season. Berlin had been absent from Broadway for more than six years, but he had returned with a varied score full of snappy, swinging songs. Ryskind, who had been in Hollywood for much of the same time, came back with "an antique point of view," wrote critic Arthur Pollock. "Ryskind was a bright young man when he left New York, but now he is a stuffy Republican, with the point of view of an after-dinner speaker." The show's success was due to Berlin's tunes, the comedy of Victor Moore, and Zorina's beauty and grace.

Berlin made it look so easy that *New York Times* critic Brooks Atkinson gently chided him by writing, "Mr. Berlin has returned to remind us that he still can write songs without bursting into a fever of perspiration," but Atkinson admired the workmanship in the whole production nonetheless. Berlin's score has come to be recognized as one of his best. Unfortunately at the time there were no such things as cast albums. Selected songs from scores would frequently be recorded by the popular singers of the period but, surprisingly, no one thought to record a show's performers singing its score. Only after the tremendous success of *Oklahoma!* three years later were shows regularly recorded. "I was always happy with *Louisiana Purchase,*" said Berlin later, "but it might have become better known if it had opened a few years later and received an original cast recording." He did find the happy medium between quality and quantity. The score's fourteen songs (plus an additional eight, which were either dropped or not used) represent a high level of consistent quality.

On a train returning from one of the show's out-of-town tryouts, Berlin talked about the war in Europe with columnist Ward Morehouse, and closed by saying

At every performance of "Louisiana Purchase," actors as well as audience find a spot here which nobody cares to miss. The wings are crowded. In foreground, just off stage, are William Gaxton, Irene Bordoni, Carol Bruce.

ABOVE: Victor Moore's comedy was one of the main ingredients in *Louisiana Purchase*'s success. His costars had as much fun watching him as the audience did. Foreground, left to right: Gaxton, Bordoni, and Bruce.

BELOW: Brother and sister Herbert and Dorothy Fields, who first thought of Ethel Merman as Annie Oakley.

OPPOSITE: The creative team of *Annie Get Your Gun*. Left to right: Josh Logan, Irving Berlin, Richard Rodgers, Oscar Hammerstein, Dorothy and Herbert Fields. Front row: Ray Middleton and Ethel Merman.

"Well if we ever get in, I'll join up if they'll let me. I'll sweep floors or write songs. I'm fifty-two, but maybe I'd be good for something." That something was *This Is the Army,* which would occupy him almost exclusively for the next two and one-half years.

After the war, Berlin considered putting together a show to employ ex-soldiers, but went to Hollywood to fulfill his obligation for *Blue Skies,* a film he had put off because of his commitments to *This Is the Army.* His relentless efforts in war, tour, and film left a tired Berlin to return to New York in the fall of 1945. Then in November a call came from Oscar Hammerstein II asking for help. Jerome Kern had died a month earlier as a result of a heart attack on Park Avenue. He had come back from Hollywood to write the music for a new show that Rodgers and Hammerstein were producing. After the team's first hit, *Oklahoma!,* they took more control of their own work, publishing their own music and producing their own shows. Their debut as producers was for another writer's work at the Music Box Theatre. In October 1944, they presented John Van Druten's drama *I Remember Mama,* a hit that ran for two years and featured the Broadway debut of Marlon Brando. They next offered a revival of Hammerstein and Kern's classic *Show Boat* in January 1946, and had hired Kern for a show that would be the first new musical they produced.

The new show was the brainchild of Dorothy Fields, who was a renowned lyricist frequently in collaboration with Jerome Kern, and her brother Herbert, who wrote the books for hit musical comedies for thirty-five years. They had the idea of casting Ethel Merman as Annie Oakley.

Rodgers remembered: "Having already chosen Kern, we felt it was extremely important to get another composer of equal stature, and this could only mean Irving Berlin. 'We're aiming awfully high to try to get Berlin,' I said to Oscar." The Fieldses were also both for asking Berlin, even if it meant that Dorothy would not write the lyrics. Berlin had his doubts, though. His idea of the West was the Beverly Wilshire Hotel, and it had been six years since his last book show. Berlin also admitted to Hammerstein that he did not feel comfortable with "hillbilly music." Hammerstein counseled him to drop the final *g* from most verbs and he would be fine. After Rodgers suggested Josh Logan as the director, Berlin was more interested, as Logan had staged some of the numbers in *This Is the Army.* Berlin read the one and only act at that point and wrote "Doin' What Comes Natur'lly" and "They Say It's Wonderful" over the weekend. He still hesitated and asked for another week to think it over. Berlin remembered that "Dick Rodgers, very rightly, said 'Why another week?,'" and Berlin was in.

Choreographer Helen Tamiris, who fused modern dance with traditional American art forms, was a natural to create stylized Indian dances (seen below in "I'm an Indian Too") and others from the Wild West. She had competing Native-American works on Broadway in the spring of 1948 when she choreographed *Inside USA* and *Annie*, which was still going strong after a year and a half.

Two decades later, Berlin recalled that the songs came quickly and easily "because of the possibilities in the Fields's script, my association with Rodgers and Hammerstein and, above all, writing songs for Ethel Merman." Merman was already a Broadway legend. After her debut in the Gershwins' *Girl Crazy*, in which she introduced "I Got Rhythm," Merman became the star of every show she was in. She had first met Berlin during the filming of *Alexander's Ragtime Band* in 1938. "I knew right away when I sang those numbers that ranged from pseudo-ragtime to swing," remembered Merman, "that Irving and I were going to work together in the future under more propitious circumstances." Merman was too big for the screen; her personality and singing had to be experienced in a space that was built for them: the theater. "I belt the lyrics over the footlights like a baseball coach belting fly balls to the outfield," said the siren. "And since I do this one basic thing, I don't have anything that you can analyze and slice thin like a 'style.'" Berlin understood that "if you write lyrics for Ethel, they had better be good; everybody's going to hear them anyhow." Berlin supplied the ammunition for Merman's firepower. The ballads made Merman feel that, as she put it, "Irving Berlin's lyrics made a lady out of me. They showed I had a softer side."

Already a living legend, Berlin was still a team player. Open production meetings for *Annie Get Your Gun* were held at

Hammerstein's home in New York, and the group ironed out many of the problems that were normally left for the out-of-town tryouts. In New Haven, Berlin may have felt odd not having any of the expected backstage dramas, and he continually reworked "Doin' What Comes Natur'lly," before leaving it as it was originally written.

For a scene played in front of the curtain while the scenery behind it changed, Berlin wrote the classic "There's No Business like Show Business." Legend has it that Berlin initially rejected the song after he felt that Rodgers and Hammerstein had not shown it much appreciation when he played the score, and he decided that it wasn't that good. Berlin did harbor doubts about his abilities as he got older. "At my age—'over twenty one'—this seems like a second helping," he wrote Harry Ruby soon after the production opened. "Every time I start on a show, I wonder if this is the time I'll reach for it and find it isn't there."

Berlin later wanted to correct the "myth" of "There's No Business like Show Business." He wrote press agent Richard Maney, who was working on the show's first revival twenty years later, "I remember calling Oscar Hammerstein and telling him the title. He was crazy about it, which of course encouraged me to write it up. Once it was in the show we all knew that it was an important part of the score. Certainly, no one, including myself, realized at that time it would become the so-called theme song for show business."

Annie proves what a good shot she is before realizing that "You Can't Get a Man with a Gun."

Mielziner and Ballard

For set designer Jo Mielziner, the 1945–1946 Broadway season was typically full of assignments. As one of the American theater's greatest designers, Mielziner was sought after by virtually every producer who wanted a fascinating yet practical concept for a set, whether it was a musical or drama, by Shakespeare or Tennessee Williams. In his more than three hundred designs, Mielziner created the look of twentieth-century Broadway.

The season began with *Carib Song,* a musical set in the West Indies, starring dancer Katherine Dunham and an African-American ensemble. Next came a four-man drama, *The Beggars Are Coming to Town,* staged by Harold Clurman. Mielziner followed this with a comedy by Elmer Rice, *Dream Girl,* a female Walter Mittyish adventure. Then came *Jeb,* an early civil rights drama that helped make Ossie Davis a star. He also designed several other shows that season that never made it to New York. Eschewing a "signature" style, Mielziner approached each show on its own terms. "If you work in the interpretative side of the theater you learn the proper relation between actor and scenery," he said. "You don't make the mistake of thinking of scenery as a picture. For a three-dimensional, realistic play, a two-dimensional set would be uninteresting, but for a stylized ballet, a flat design would be good."

When possible, he liked to work one-on-one with the playwright to make the set serve the play as much as possible.

For his final production of the season, he was reunited with Rodgers and Hammerstein. Mielziner had designed a number of Rodgers and Hart productions in the 1930s, and while he had missed the chance to work with the team on *Oklahoma!,* he had designed their *Carousel* the previous season. This time he worked for them in their roles as producers of *Annie Get Your Gun.*

The nine sets for the show ranged from a Pullman car to the ballroom of New York's grand Hotel Brevoort and were a mixture of painted drops and fully furnished spaces. Mielziner understood that the metaphor of the production was show business and he gave each set a theatrical look. As with many of his assignments, he designed the lighting as well, manipulating the actual performing space without changing sets.

Nevertheless, the show gave him a reputation of creating heavy sets. When the show was loaded into the Imperial, a steel beam broke. The set seemed to be too heavy for the stage gridiron. Since the theater infrastructure was damaged,

ABOVE: Ballard's designs for *Annie*'s performance costumes.

LEFT: Mielziner's study for "I'm an Indian Too."

an out-of-town booking was hastily arranged in Philadelphia. Eventually it was discovered that there was a structural defect in the beam. But Mielziner's reputation was tainted by the incident.

Costume designer Lucinda Ballard was also a Rodgers and Hammerstein regular, designing six of their productions, from *I Remember Mama* to *The Sound of Music*. The wife of lyricist and director Howard Dietz, Ballard was a classically trained artist who, like Mielziner, worked to fit her six-time Tony-winning designs into the production, rather than creating costumes that looked beautiful but had no relation to the show.

From songwriting to set design, the legendary talents responsible for *Annie Get Your Gun* produced a rare show. Each created elements that were great examples of their craft, yet also integral to the overall production.

BELOW: Mielziner's rendering of the Wild West show in which Annie performs.

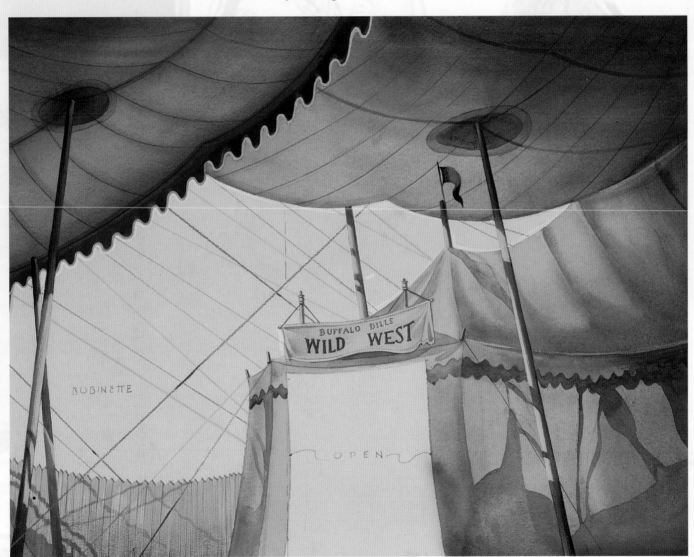

Annie Get Your Gun was an unqualified hit, with Merman and Berlin receiving much of the praise. Berlin was confident by opening night, in part because he had faith in the audience's review of his songs. "When you write for a Broadway show, you get to know very quickly if they like them." As compared to the lengthy time between songwriting and performance in film production, he knew that in the theater you swiftly "get the satisfaction of hearing them sung." On opening night, Berlin wired set designer Jo Mielziner: "GOOD LUCK, JO. I DON'T THINK WE HAVE MUCH TO WORRY ABOUT." All Merman's telegram to Berlin said was "THANKS."

The success of *Annie Get Your Gun* energized Berlin. Only six months later, the film *Blue Skies* was released and was a hit. Berlin felt rejuvenated. Although he never again would write a complete new score for a film (a distinction he saved for Broadway), he returned to Hollywood in 1947 to make *Easter Parade* at MGM. The studio also won the rights to film *Annie Get Your Gun* as a vehicle for Judy Garland, but a series of mishaps delayed its completion until 1950 starring Betty Hutton. In 1948 Berlin began to work on a score for a new Broadway show with Norman Krasna, *Stars on My Shoulders.* The book never satisfied anyone, and pieces of the score would later end up in the 1954 film *White Christmas.*

OPPOSITE: Almost every show or film that Berlin worked on had some element of show business about it. "There's No Business Like Show Business," which he wrote for the score of *Annie Get Your Gun,* summed up a lifetime of working in the trade, from vaudeville to Broadway to Hollywood.

BELOW: Ethel Merman and Ray Middleton take aim in the rousing finale of *Annie Get Your Gun.*

Berlin regretted a cast album was not standard practice at the time of *Louisiana Purchase.* For *Miss Liberty,* he recorded a series of demos for Columbia singers before the show opened. After opening, the cast, including Eddie Albert and Allyn Ann McLerie, shown here, assembled at Columbia's studios for the show's original cast recording.

While in London to check on the West End production of *Annie Get Your Gun,* Berlin visited his old Round Table friend, Robert Sherwood, who lived in Surrey. Sherwood had won the Pulitzer Prize three times for dramas, including *Abe Lincoln in Illinois* and *Idiot's Delight,* the latter featuring Alfred Lunt as a second-string hoofer singing "Puttin' on the Ritz." During the war, Sherwood had worked for President Roosevelt, and had also just won a Pulitzer Prize for his book *Roosevelt and Hopkins.* Only two years earlier, he had won the Oscar for best screenplay for *The Best Years of Our Lives.* Although he had never written a musical before, he proposed to Berlin that they collaborate on a musical comedy on the origins of the Statue of Liberty.

Perhaps the idea appealed to Berlin's aesthetic and business instincts. Besides the flag, nothing symbolized America like the Statue of Liberty, and as Sherwood told him the story of its creation, it seemed ripe for a musical treatment. Originally, the romance in the story was to come from the French model who posed for the statue, but Berlin's research had uncovered the inconvenient fact that sculptor Bartholdi's mother posed for the work. Sherwood responded by dreaming up a story in which a hapless newspaper photographer (Eddie Albert) goes to Paris to take a picture of the model, and mistakes a young woman (Allyn Ann McLerie) in the sculptor's studio as the one. Since neither is fluent in the other's native tongue, she doesn't understand when the photographer insists on bringing her to America as a coup for his newspaper, *The New York Herald.* The rivalry between the *Herald* and Joseph Pulitzer's *World* is a subplot in the story. The libretto got fairly complicated at points and lacked a sense of humor, so important in the period when "musical" meant musical comedy. If Berlin was concerned, he felt that rehearsals and out-of-town tryouts could fix things. Berlin and Sherwood had decided to produce the show themselves, with Josh Logan, who would also direct. Again Berlin worked quickly on the score, but soon realized that if Logan was going to be involved, they would have to wait until he completed his commitment to Rodgers and Hammerstein's *South Pacific.* This would make them miss their desired July Fourth opening.

Instead, Berlin turned to Moss Hart, fresh from being nominated for an Oscar for adapting *Gentlemen's Agreement,* and experiencing a modest success with a back-stage comedy about an out-of-town tryout, *Light Up the Sky.* Hart would also join as a producer. As with *Annie Get Your Gun,* the trio rounded out the team with some of the best creative minds in the business, including Jerome Robbins as choreographer, Oliver Smith as set designer, and the three women collectively known as Motley as the show's costume designer.

ABOVE: Longtime performer Ethel Griffies stole the show when she sang "Only for Americans."

LEFT: Eddie Albert mistakes Allyn Ann McLerie as the model for the Statue of Liberty when he finds her in sculptor Bartholdi's studio.

When choreographer Jerome Robbins heard of the creative team being assembled for *Miss Liberty*, he told his agent, "Get me that." Robbins's choreography enlivened the show, even though his best dance, the sultry "Mr. Monotony," was cut. Although Robbins (seen here rehearsing with Allyn Ann McLerie, above right) felt the conventional book provided him little to work with, he was inspired by Berlin's score, including "The Policeman's Ball" (below left) and "Paris Wakes Up and Smiles" (below right). Robbins would team with Berlin for their next Broadway show, *Call Me Madam*, in 1950.

Rehearsals began on May 13, 1949, in New York and the first preview was set for Philadelphia exactly one month later. In the ever-superstitious theater community, there were those who questioned the wisdom of starting on the show on the thirteenth, let alone Friday the thirteenth. "This is a show about the United States, and anybody concerned with the states shouldn't consider thirteen an unlucky number," Sherwood told columnist Leonard Lyons, comparing the show to the country's colonial beginnings, "because that's what we started with."

Miss Liberty, as the show was called, had an air of success due to its pedigree and subject matter. Berlin was so enthusiastic about the score that he took his piano to Columbia Recording Studios to make a demo disk of all the tunes so that they could be passed around to Columbia artists to perform. Many Broadway first-nighters were already planning on attending the Philadelphia opening to witness history in the making.

Oliver Smith's style and imagination covered a wide range of plays and periods beginning with *Rosalinda* in 1942 through *My Fair Lady, West Side Story,* and *Hello Dolly!* He used painted flats for *Miss Liberty* and incorporated the proscenium to create a vivid tableau that suggested a newspaper photograph.

Unfortunately, the book did not improve. Sherwood was reluctant to change the text and was simply unable to adapt to writing for musical comedy. A week after the Philadelphia opening, Sherwood described the claustrophobia he felt

Elizabeth Montgomery, Margaret Harris, and Sophia Harris made up Motley, a unique costume- and scene-design studio located first in London's West End and then on Broadway for more than forty years. The studio provided designs for many shows, including *South Pacific*, *Peter Pan*, and *Long Day's Journey into Night*. For *Miss Liberty*, Motley created nearly two hundred women's costumes (each requiring a hat and a pair of gloves), and more than 160 hats for the men. For inspiration, they turned to nineteenth-century French painters. The demimonde of Toulouse-Lautrec's work was brought to life for "Only the Americans," and the style of Renoir influenced "Let's Take an Old-Fashioned Walk." As beautiful as the set was, one reviewer wrote that "it is still eclipsed by Motley's costuming."

writing for *Miss Liberty* with seventeen songs in the score, "There I am with Berlin to the right of me, Berlin to the left of me, Berlin in front of me, Berlin behind. Frankly I am surrounded by Berlin." The writer of serious dramas also recognized that the show lacked humor. "At first it was difficult for me to get comedy in it; there's no chance to develop natural comic situations—there's no time for it, no room for it. And I can't write jokes. The show seems to be gay and good natured, but it wasn't easy to get uproarious laughter into it."

Due to expectations, the show's box-office receipts were good, and the producing triumvirate decided to keep it out of New York for an additional week, thereby sacrificing their July Fourth opening on Broadway. But the revisions did not make a big difference. The situation was later described as the story of "how five geniuses can make one turkey." Berlin knew the contest for audiences would be tough. After two weeks of rehearsals, he wired his friend Cole Porter, who was enjoying the success of *Kiss Me Kate,* which had opened in December of 1948, "THERE'S A LOT OF COMPETITION AROUND THESE DAYS AND I'M LOOKING STRAIGHT AT YOU."

The show had the misfortune of opening after another highlight of the American musical theater, Rodgers and Hammerstein's *South Pacific.* Against these two shows, a good score and a lousy book were not enough to excite critics, who labeled the show "routine." Brooks Atkinson wrote that the show was "bogged down in the clichés of old-fashioned musical comedy." He concluded by writing, "In view of their special gifts as writers, they have missed the opportunity of their Broadway careers."

For Sherwood, it was the end of his work on Broadway, although he revised a Phillip Barry play, *Second Threshold,* two years later. It would be seven years before Moss Hart would work on another Broadway musical, the seemingly hopeless project of turning Shaw's *Pygmalion* into a show (eventually called *My Fair Lady*).

Miss Liberty was enough of a hit with audiences to run almost a year and support a modest national tour. Berlin, who started work on his next Broadway offering the month after *Miss Liberty* opened, wrote conductor Jay Blackton in February of 1950, "I keep getting all the news, mostly bad, about 'Miss Liberty,' but frankly I am not worried about it. I have given it my all and feel that we have not done too badly with something that was not too good." Berlin had little, in fact, to worry about. He had enjoyed a string of hits in Hollywood during the 1940s. The next decade would see a few more added to his list, and there would be an unqualified Broadway hit as well.

TOP: Moss Hart, director and producer of *Miss Liberty*. He would go on to direct *My Fair Lady* in 1956.

ABOVE: Designers Elizabeth Montgomery and Oliver Smith at rehearsals for *Miss Liberty*.

After returning to America from his exhausting tour of the South Pacific, Berlin went to Hollywood. Mark Sandrich, Berlin's most consistently sympathetic director, died ten days into preproduction of *Blue Skies.* Conceived in the fall of 1942 to assuage Berlin and Sandrich after they learned that they would not work together on the film of *This Is the Army,* the production was put off until late winter 1945. Meant to be a reunion of the creative team of *Holiday Inn,* instead it became a variation on that film.

Berlin worried that age might have dulled his talent. Comparing the effort required for film work to his stage scores, Berlin wrote to a friend in 1946, "It's different with a movie. I know that racket pretty well and no matter how hard or how long you have to work, it's pretty sure-fire—that is, commercially—it's all been done before and you're not sticking your neck out quite so far." Over the next eight years he made six films, including adaptations of two of his Broadway hits. The scores were collections of both new and old songs. The films are among his best known, with remarkable performances by Astaire, Crosby, Donald O'Connor, Ethel Merman, Danny Kaye, Rosemary Clooney, Marilyn Monroe, and Judy Garland.

Filming the Five Donohues' reunion in the final scene of *There's No Business Like Show Business.*

HOLLYWOOD
1945-1954

1945

1946

March 4 Mark Sandrich dies of a heart attack in his home at age forty-four.

March 24 Berlin returns home from the South Pacific tour of *This Is the Army*.

June Berlin and family spend the summer in Beverly Hills.

August *Blue Skies* (Paramount) starts filming.

October 10 *The Jolson Story* is released, with Larry Parks lip-synching to a new Jolson performance of "Let Me Sing and I'm Happy."

October 16 *Blue Skies* is released. The film becomes the highest grosser of Astaire's career. Berlin's "You Keep Coming Back like a Song" is nominated for an Academy Award, as is Robert Dolan's music direction.

1953

1954

1957

August *White Christmas* (Paramount) begins filming.

October 14 *White Christmas*, the first film in Paramount's Vista Vision (the company's answer to CinemaScope), is released. Berlin receives his final Oscar nomination for "Count Your Blessings Instead of Sheep."

December 16 *There's No Business Like Show Business* (Twentieth Century–Fox) is released.

December 5 *Sayonara*, for which Berlin wrote the title tune, is released.

1947   1948   1950   1953

June The Berlins rent a house in Santa Monica for the summer. Working with screenwriters Albert and Frances Hackett, Berlin begins preparations for *Easter Parade*.

November 25 *Easter Parade* starts filming.

June 30 *Easter Parade* (MGM) premieres. According to Berlin, "The one person responsible for the whole musical context of the picture was Roger Edens." Edens and Johnny Green win an Oscar for their music direction.

May 17 *Annie Get Your Gun* (MGM) released. Roger Edens and Adolph Deutsch win Academy Award for music direction. The picture also receives nominations for cinematography and editing.

March 25 *Call Me Madam* (Twentieth Century–Fox) premieres. Irene Sharaff's costume designs are nominated, but only Alfred Newman's music direction wins an Academy Award.

Call Me Madam's film cast sings out. Left to right: George Sanders, Billy De Wolfe, Ethel Merman, Donald O'Connor, and Vera-Ellen.

YOU KEEP COMING
BACK LIKE A SONG

*"Show business isn't just scenery, lights, greasepaint and glitter, it's
heart. Because, if your show hasn't got heart, you haven't got a show."*

Irving Berlin, 1954

At the end of February 1945, Mark Sandrich invited two young Hollywood performers, dancer Paul Draper and actress Joan Caulfield, to his home for lunch, to talk about *Blue Skies.* The film, which they were just about to start shooting, centered on a catalogue of new and old Irving Berlin songs. This was a big break for Caulfield. Sandrich had reportedly seen the dailies of her first film and, struck by her beauty, gave her a starring role in the picture, Paramount's most expensive movie to date ($3 million). More likely, it was the star of *Blue Skies,* Bing Crosby, who was struck by her beauty and asked her to be cast. It was the beginning of an affair that would last several years.

Sandrich had plucked Draper from his success in New York nightclubs, and signed him to a long-term contract. As both producer and director, Sandrich perhaps recognized that the talent of this unknown could win a film audience. Nothing would indicate that in two weeks Sandrich would no longer be in the picture, dead of a heart attack at age forty-four.

Berlin had already provided the scenario, and contributed four new songs. He had fulfilled the terms of his contract but felt he had a moral obligation to come out immediately to help, as well as to protect his investment. Bing Crosby, the biggest name in American entertainment at that time, was still involved, and the story was a variation on *Holiday Inn,* in which partners split up over the love of a girl. The dancer goes to Hollywood, and Crosby, who gets the girl, infuriates her by opening a series of theme-related nightclubs all over the country instead of settling down in one place. When filming

Astaire and Bing Crosby clown around in "A Couple of Song-and-Dance Men" from *Blue Skies.*

Fred Astaire in his costume for "Heat Wave" in *Blue Skies* (1946).

ABOVE: Crosby and Joan Caulfield huddle together when the blue skies he was singing about turn rainy.

RIGHT: Crosby's Johnny Adams's nightclub, The Songbook, where he sings "You Keep Coming Back like a Song" and wins back Mary O'Hara, played by Joan Caulfield.

OPPOSITE: The "Puttin' on the Ritz" number was the result of "Five weeks of backbreaking physical work," according to Astaire. It was to be his "last dance."

did begin in the summer, Draper was replaced because of a stammer in his speech (and his reluctance to work with Caulfield, an inexperienced dancer). Berlin and the studio felt they needed a performer of Crosby's stature for his screen partner.

Fred Astaire, who had previously turned down the part, accepted the role on the second request. At forty-seven, Astaire had been in show business for more than forty years and felt creatively exhausted. He believed dancing was "eighty percent brain work and twenty percent footwork," and was not anxious to repeat himself or do mediocre work. "I made up my mind during the shooting of this film that I wanted to retire on it," wrote Astaire later. "*Blue Skies* measured up to the requirements I considered essential: It looked like a hit."

Astaire saved the picture. His performance, especially a solo set to "Puttin' on the Ritz," which he said would be his last dance, is one of his masterpieces. Over a slow version of the song with a new lyric, Astaire makes his cane come to life before he starts to perform with eight mirror images of himself. Most of his dances in the film are solos because of his last-minute addition to the cast. Berlin saw this as a positive when the film came out. "[Astaire] didn't have time to plan and rehearse the routines with Joan Caulfield or, except for that one number ("Heat Wave"), with Olga St. Juan. That turned out to be very good for the picture. If he'd been in from the start, as we'd hoped, we'd have written a more conventional

In his new Top Hat nightclub, Crosby sings "Everybody Step."

picture. Astaire would have danced with the girl, as he usually does. Now he dances by himself. And I think it's grand."

The intensely private Berlin must have also been happy that this cavalcade of songs was not based on his biography, a fate that had befallen his friend Cole Porter. Porter was the subject of Warners' *Night and Day,* a biopic starring Cary Grant that was being made at the same time. *The New York Times*'s Bosley Crowther pointed out that musicals filled with many of a single composer's songs are usually biographies, but this film was free to spin anything, including fiction. In *Blue Skies,* with twenty-eight songs in a 104-minute film, there was, on average, a Berlin song every four minutes, which did not leave time for much of a story to be developed. What is on show is decidedly mediocre until Astaire starts to dance or Crosby starts to sing.

Berlin knew *Blue Skies* was not perfect, but it had been salvaged. Before the opening he said, "This kind of picture is rather like a party. If I start to pick a picture to pieces I can find all kinds of flaws. That is true of a party. Maybe you have to throw out a couple of drunks, but afterwards you forget that—you just remember you had a grand time." His instincts were right. Despite tepid reviews, the film was one of the biggest-grossing films of the year.

With the success of *Blue Skies* on film and *Annie Get Your Gun* on Broadway, Berlin knew he was in the position to get what he wanted. He suggested to his old friend Joe Schenck a film that would follow the same formula as *Blue Skies,* with new songs for the film's stars, as well as some from the Berlin catalogue. Schenck went to his bosses at Fox, who were anxious to do the picture but refused to give a percentage of the film's profits to the songwriter. So Berlin took the project to MGM, and Louis B. Mayer eventually agreed to his terms. They envisioned a film to be called *Easter Parade,* starring Judy Garland and Gene Kelly, who was his generation's ideal dancer as the older Astaire was his. Berlin was excited about working with Garland. "She's got something all the great ones had, the great ones I can remember. She's got the thing that made Nora Bayes great, and Al Jolson. It's the way she sings, the way she puts over a song. Besides that, she's got a great talent."

Albert and Francis Hackett were assigned to write the script as a backstage story set in the vaudeville/Ziegfeld era of 1911–1912, a part of American cultural history Berlin knew well. He had lived through the era, not simply as an observer but as a participant.

"I think you might fit into my show!"

LEFT: Films in the first half of the twentieth century were publicized through myriad forms of printed ephemera. Here is a "lobby card," one of a set of usually eight cards for a theater lobby, with *Easter Parade*'s four principal performers: Peter Lawford, Ann Miller, Fred Astaire, and Judy Garland. Most of the cast changed right before filming, with Astaire replacing Gene Kelly and Ann Miller replacing Cyd Charisse, yet there is a palpable on-screen chemistry among the actors.

Originally Vincente Minnelli, a great musical director and Garland's husband, was to have directed the film. After Garland's doctors suggested that the stress of living and working together might be too much for the performer, producer Arthur Freed replaced Minnelli with choreographer-turned-director Charles Walters. Walters brought Sidney Sheldon in for rewrites, which included making Kelly's character more likable, and the production was ready to begin.

Right before filming started, Kelly broke his ankle playing touch football and had to withdraw. He suggested Astaire, who was induced to end his "retirement" by the thought of working with Judy Garland. Astaire had come to the rescue again for Berlin. Cyd Charisse, who was to play the "other woman" in the picture, tore her knee ligaments on the set of the film she was just finishing, so she was replaced right before filming by Ann Miller. These setbacks turned into major assets for *Easter Parade.* Astaire's easygoing grace suffused the film with a bonhomie that brought out the best in his costars. Garland, struggling with depression, looked forward to her work and developed an on-screen chemistry with Astaire that belied their twenty-three-year difference in age.

Berlin was inspired by his cast. For Astaire he wrote "Steppin' Out with My Baby," which quickly became a standard. That number was to be followed by Garland singing a new torch song, "Mr. Monotony," which stopped the action of the film. Berlin would try to use it on Broadway in his

ABOVE: In the office that producer Arthur Freed permanently renamed the Berlin Room, the songwriter wrote out the lyrics to a new song, "It Only Happens When I Dance with You" (right).

OPPOSITE: When Freed rejected "Let's Take an Old-Fashioned Walk," Berlin went back and wrote out another new song, "A Couple of Swells," which would become a standard. Garland would revive this number for her nightclub act.

next two shows (and in another film), but each time it was not right and was cut. Forty-two years later it would finally make its debut in *Jerome Robbins' Broadway*.

Easter Parade sports the rich look of MGM musicals, culminating in a scene on Fifth Avenue during the Easter Parade of 1912. It was only the third color film that Berlin had worked on and he was lucky to have art direction that gave it a rosy glow. Berlin had wanted a more realistic plot, but despite Sidney Sheldon's somewhat hackneyed script, he said soon after the film opened, "I've always despised that constant effort in the theater and pictures to be unique and original. A picture or a play is good or bad. So is a song. If they're also different, O.K. But it's a great mistake to set out with no objective but being unusual. No, this picture isn't spectacularly inventive at all. It's another backstage story, but it's done well and the ingredients are individually good." For Berlin, backstage stories were the best choice for musicals. "Outside of fantasies, which permit any liberties, it's still the most logical way to account for showgirls coming from no-place, large orchestras sneaking in to accompany vocals, and big production numbers. I say again, don't knock it just because it ain't new."

ABOVE: Garland and Astaire stroll down Fifth Avenue at the conclusion of *Easter Parade*.

RIGHT: "The WACs who dressed in slacks/Dancing cheek to cheek and pants to pants." From "Gee, I Wish I Was Back in the Army," in *White Christmas*.

Clearly, Berlin had this in mind when he started his next original project, a film based on the most popular song in America, "White Christmas." His original scenario took bits of the *Holiday Inn* story and pieces of the unrealized musical he had written with Norman Krasna, *Stars on My Shoulder,* and envisioned a story starring Crosby, Astaire, Ginger Rogers, and "another younger girl, perhaps Debbie Reynolds." Krasna would eventually write the script, which had a singing and dancing team of ex-G.I.s who find that their beloved general from their war years now runs an inn in Vermont that he is in danger of losing owing to three consecutive winters without snow (here Berlin mixed a backstage story with fantasy). The team rallies their soldier friends and, along with a sister act they have met in New York, come and save the day for the general. They put on a big show that also coincides with a snowstorm.

Rogers was never seriously connected with the project, nor was Reynolds, but Astaire and Crosby were signed, with Crosby as a producer along with Berlin and Paramount. For the female leads they signed singer Rosemary Clooney and dancer Vera-Ellen. Astaire got sick right

Berlin took the music to the unused "Free" from *Call Me Madam* and wrote a new lyric. The song, retitled "Snow," is sung by the four leads as they take a train to Vermont in *White Christmas*.

before preproduction and was replaced by Donald O'Connor. Then, just as filming was about to begin, O'Connor also became ill and was likely to be sidelined for months. The producers approached Danny Kaye, who asked for a then-exorbitant sum ($200,000 plus 10 percent of the gross), expecting to be turned down. After calculating that delaying the film for O'Connor would cost them almost as much, they signed him in less than forty-eight hours. Berlin changed the title and lyrics of "A Singer—A Dancer" to "A Crooner—A Comic," but otherwise left his score intact. Among the new songs, "Count Your Blessings" was nominated for an Academy Award and "Love, You Didn't Do Right by Me" (sung by Clooney in the film), has enjoyed some success in cabaret.

Just as filming started, Berlin wrote to his longtime friend Irving Hoffman, "It is the first movie that I've been connected with since 'Holiday Inn' that has the feel of a Broadway musical. Usually there's little enthusiasm once you get over the first week of a picture. But the change in this setup has resulted in an excitement that I am sure will be reflected in the finished job. In any event, as of today I feel great and very much like an opening in Philadelphia with a show."

As he had written Harry Ruby eight years earlier, he knew how to work on a picture. He needed to risk little creatively for a return that would be great. Again, his instincts were right and the film became one of the biggest hits of 1954, and since has become a holiday favorite. He savored this success as he worked on what would be his last film, another picture titled after one of his best-known songs, *There's No Business like Show Business*.

Four years earlier, Berlin had tried to interest MGM in a new project. He wrote producer Eddie Mannix, "Incidentally, in my contract with Metro for 'Annie' I have the right to use any title of the score for a motion picture and the use of that song in that picture three years after 'Annie' is released. I've thought for a long time that 'There's No Business like Show Business' is a great title and the theme for a big back-stage musical using all the stars in the studio." He had wanted to work out a three-picture deal, but MGM seems not to have pursued the idea.

For Berlin, especially as he got older, the tried and true was the best course, so he returned to Fox again. Zanuck wrote in the outline of the story, "Here is the story of a family we are thinking about . . . they are not Barrymores, but they are people who, for two or three or even four generations, have been in the business— who know nothing else—who think, talk, eat and sleep nothing but theater . . . they are Irish . . . they are a fighting, sentimental, humorous, lovable and loving group of people . . . they have something in common with the O'Learys in *In Old Chicago*,

AL HIRSCHFELD

ABOVE: The Berlins found Mr. and Mrs. Bennett Cerf with John O'Hara at Lindy's after the opening of *White Christmas* in New York.

OPPOSITE: Betty Hutton replaced Judy Garland in the film adaptation of *Annie Get Your Gun.*

with the family in *You Can't Take It with You,* with the family in *Mother Wore Tights.*"

The film centers on a husband and wife vaudeville team who integrate their three children into the act, and their subsequent trials and tribulations, including the appearance of a rising starlet whom one son falls for. The other son leaves the act to become a priest. For Berlin, it may have seemed like he had come full circle. In *The Jazz Singer,* Jolson's character leaves the world of religion for show business. Here the opposite was true. And if *The Jazz Singer* celebrated the theater, the new film depicted its dissolution, as the finale marks the closing of the venerable Hippodrome Theatre.

Ethel Merman was cast as the mother. When Berlin saw Marilyn Monroe's photo at Joe Schenck's house, he was seized by the idea that she represented the 1950s as Merman had personified the 1930s. He had the idea that each would sing "Heat Wave." In the film, Merman is to sing it with her family in a big revue, but

ABOVE: Mitzi Gaynor plays Katy Donohue, a singer and dancer, in *There's No Business like Show Business.*

RIGHT: Ethel Merman and Dan Dailey play Molly and Terry Donohue, a couple on the vaudeville circuit.

OPPOSITE, TOP: Johnny Ray sings "If You Believe," a song Berlin originally wrote for *Reaching for the Moon* nearly a quarter century before.

OPPOSITE, BOTTOM: The Donohues introduce their children to the audience after singing "Simple Melody."

OVERLEAF: Marilyn Monroe sings "Lazy" with Gaynor and Donald O'Connor in a rehearsal for the revue within the film.

IRVING BERLIN'S SHOW BUSINESS

Monroe goes on and gives it a very sultry reading that brings down the house. Again, the symbol of the new triumphs over the old. Although Monroe was not at first interested in the picture, she was induced to join the cast when Zanuck dangled as bait the chance for the lead in *The Seven-Year Itch.*

In a letter to music director Alfred Newman, Berlin even considered appearing in a cameo at the start of the film, playing "Remember" on his transposing piano. Berlin agreed with Newman that the sentiments of that song were the real theme of the picture, and certainly the theme of all of Berlin's later films. At sixty-six, having worked for nearly a half century, Berlin had given audiences a great deal to remember. In his note, Berlin recalled that he had introduced Newman to Hollywood in 1930 when they worked on *Reaching for the Moon,* and reminded him that the song "If You Believe" in the new film was originally written for that 1930 debacle.

Some of the songs in the film had been written so much earlier that the Fox publicity department mistakenly touted the 1920s "After You Get What You Want,

IRVING BERLIN'S SHOW BUSINESS

You Don't Want It," which is Monroe's first song in the movie, as a "new" song. The score only had two "new" songs, one that had been written six years earlier for *Stars on My Shoulder,* "A Man Chases a Girl (Until She Catches Him)," and "A Sailor's Not a Sailor (Till a Sailor's Been Tattooed)," an old-time production number sung in a vaudeville-act setting by Merman and her screen daughter, Mitzi Gaynor. Berlin's first song in the movies, "Blue Skies" in *The Jazz Singer,* was fresh from the dominant form of entertainment, Broadway. His last film showed how antiquated the theater could be. Yet only Irving Berlin had spanned the complete spectrum, conquering each new medium as it arose. *There's No Business like Show Business* added another hit to Berlin's box-office tally. He felt that despite nineteen films with complete Berlin scores, and dozens of others that had featured one or more songs, he retained his most valuable property to turn into a blockbuster film: *Say It with Music,* the story of the Music Box Theatre.

After mining American history in his last two Broadway productions, Berlin returned to American politics for his remaining two shows. For both shows he collaborated with the playwriting team of Howard Lindsay and Russel Crouse, who had been Broadway fixtures since their first success as the book-writers for Cole Porter's *Anything Goes* in 1934. In the intervening fifteen years, they had written a score of hits, including the longest-running play in Broadway history, *Life with Father,* and the Pulitzer Prize–winning *State of the Union.*

Their political instinct was just right in 1950 for *Call Me Madam,* a show that spoofed America's postwar wealth and influence. The show, starring Ethel Merman, was both a hit on Broadway and, with its screen adaptation, in movie theaters; and with "They Like Ike," Berlin gave one presidential candidate a theme song. But after a twelve-year hiatus from Broadway, Berlin failed to find the right tune for the fictional commander-in-chief at the center of *Mr. President.* Written while the country basked in the promise of the Kennedy administration, the show felt like a lame duck.

Raoul Pène du Bois's rendering for Dean Acheson's office in *Call Me Madam,* 1950.

BROADWAY
1950–1962

Berlin tries out a new number for
Call Me Madam's star Ethel Merman.

1950

1952

October 12 *Call Me Madam* opens at the Imperial Theatre. It runs for 644 performances and wins four Tony Awards, including Best Original Score, Best Actress in a Musical, and Best Featured Actor in a Musical.

May 3 *Call Me Madam* closes on Broadway. After Merman performs in the first national tour stop in Washington, Elaine Stritch takes over the role.

THIS IS A GREAT COUNTRY

LELAND HAYWARD
presents

ROBERT
RYAN

NANETTE
FABRAY

in

Mr. President

A NEW MUSICAL COMEDY

Music and Lyrics by
IRVING BERLIN

Book by
HOWARD LINDSAY and RUSSEL CROUSE

Directed by
JOSHUA LOGAN

with
ANITA GILLETTE   JACK HASKELL
JACK WASHBURN   STANLEY GROVER   JERRY STRICKLER   WISA D'ORSO

Settings & Lighting by JO MIELZINER   Costumes Supervised by THEONI V. ALDREDGE
Choreography by PETER GENNARO   Musical Direction by JAY BLACKTON
Orchestrations by PHILIP J. LANG
Dance Music Arranged and Orchestrated by JACK ELLIOTT

ORIGINAL CAST ALBUM BY COLUMBIA RECORDS

$1.00

Also published separately from the score:
IS HE THE ONLY MAN IN THE WORLD • IN OUR HIDE-AWAY • PIGTAILS AND FRECKLES • IT
GETS LONELY IN THE WHITE HOUSE • THEY LOVE ME • MEAT AND POTATOES • THE WASHING-
TON TWIST • DON'T BE AFRAID OF ROMANCE • LAUGH IT UP • LET'S GO BACK TO THE WALTZ
• GLAD TO BE HOME • THIS IS A GREAT COUNTRY • EMPTY POCKETS FILLED WITH LOVE

© Copyright 1962 Irving Berlin

IRVING BERLIN
Music Corporation
1290 AVENUE OF AMERICAS, NEW YORK, N.Y. 10019

As was his practice, Berlin sings the entire score for the cast on the first day of rehearsals for *Mr. President*.

 1962   1963

October 20 *Mr. President* opens at the St. James Theatre on Broadway. Tony nominations go to Nanette Fabray (Best Actress in a Musical) and Jay Blackton (Best Conductor and Musical Director), but only Solly Pernick wins, for Best Stage Technician.

June 8 *Mr. President* closes after 265 performances.

YOU GOT TO BE
WAY OUT TO BE IN

"Lindsay and Irving Berlin to dinner and tell him our idea," playwright Russel Crouse confided to his diary on August 22, 1949, "and he's never heard of Perle Mesta and doesn't know much about square dancing. And I am discouraged but he warms up later." Lindsay and Crouse had thought up a new idea for a musical based on the exploits of Perle Mesta, a wealthy manufacturer's widow who had moved to Washington a decade earlier and raised money for the Democratic Party. She entertained the cream of the political and business worlds in her home and was well known for her lively charm and lightheartedness. After Truman's reelection in 1948, to which she was a substantial contributer, Mesta was appointed the first female ambassador to the duchy of Luxembourg. Lindsay and Crouse thought a straight-talking American abroad in the Old World had potential, and they felt that Ethel Merman would be perfect in a musical about Mesta entitled *Call Me Madam*.

Although Mesta was familiar to many Americans, that number did not include either Merman or Berlin. Once they had described Mesta to Merman she thought the show was a good idea, but was not sure she wanted to do another musical. She was anxious to try a dramatic role, but Lindsay convinced her to sing "a few songs." Merman then suggested Berlin as the ideal composer. For a show with a real American theme, there was no one better than Berlin.

After Ellin told him who Mesta was, Berlin called Crouse the next day, enthused about the project. That winter Berlin went to Nassau and wrote half of the score, including two of the best numbers in the show, "The Hostess with Mostes' on the Ball" and "Can You Use Any Money Today?" Yet he began to worry that at sixty-one he could longer "reach up there" and find new songs. Once he got Lindsay and Crouse to simplify the story, the remaining songs came quickly. "I've tried to work completely from their book. The songs I've written are topical enough to be in a revue. The show

Berlin and Merman confer during rehearsals of *Call Me Madam*.

When told that Mainbocher was to design her gowns for the show, Merman said, "This is like going to God."

ABOVE: Hirschfeld saw that for Lindsay and Crouse, their work was literally an act. The team noted in the program that "neither the character of Mrs. Sally Adams nor Miss Ethel Merman resemble any person living or dead." They set the show "in two mythical countries. One is called Lichtenburg. The other is the United States."

BELOW: *Call Me Madam*'s creative team (left to right): set and costume designer Raoul Pène du Bois, producer Leland Hayward, Howard Lindsay, George Abbott, Russel Crouse, Ethel Merman, Irving Berlin, and male lead Paul Lukas.

is as topical as *State of the Union,*" Berlin said right before *Call Me Madam* opened, referring to Lindsay and Crouse's comic hit about life in the White House. "The songs I've done are certainly not for the 'Annie' type of show. I've tried not to write for Ethel Merman but for the situations that the boys have provided. I'm sure that Ethel can sing any song I've written—but it better be good." Six months after he had first heard about the idea for the show, Berlin had apparently finished the score and played Merman her songs. "Irving Berlin called to say that Ethel loves the songs," Crouse wrote in his diary on March 14, 1950, "and gets [sic] on to confirm this in true Merman fashion."

Leland Hayward, fresh from his success with *South Pacific,* agreed to produce and George Abbott was signed to direct. Abbott had been in the theater almost as long as Berlin, first as a performer and then as a director (and sometimes author), who had staged such historic shows as *Room Service, Three Men on a Horse* (which he also wrote), *On Your Toes* (for which he was also the librettist), *Pal Joey,* and *Where's Charley?* (for which he also wrote the book). In the crisp, swift-paced direction of his shows, Abbott literally had no peer.

Abbott had wanted to hire George Balanchine to choreograph the show but knew that Berlin was less than enthusiastic, confirming in a letter in May 1950, "I know you feel he was barely adequate in *Louisiana Purchase.*" They settled on Jerome Robbins, whose work had been one of the highlights of *Miss Liberty.* Robbins was one of the outstanding choreographers on Broadway. His "Fancy Free" ballet had been transformed into a musical, the classic *On the Town,* only five years

earlier. What would be his best-known work lay in the future: choreographing and/or directing shows such as *The King and I, Peter Pan, West Side Story, Gypsy,* and *Fiddler on the Roof.*

Robbins eagerly accepted the chance to reunite with Berlin, and had worked with Abbott before on a number of shows. While Robbins's brash personality meant that he often clashed with his collaborators, he was very respectful of both Abbott and Berlin. Abbott recalled in his memoirs that for *Call Me Madam* "[Robbins] had conceived a big number about the wild men from the mountains coming down and dancing in the village. Eventually this number had to be jettisoned. Time and time again the ambitious dance effort will fail, whereas something conceived for practical purposes and on the spur of the moment will be a success. This is equally true of song."

In New Haven, Berlin found out how right Abbott had been. *Call Me Madam*'s second act had "a big hole," according to Berlin, so he decided to try fitting in a song he had first written for *Easter Parade,* and had tried again to include in *Miss Liberty*: "Mr. Monotony." Robbins's staging of the number in the last show had been terrific, and it hurt everyone to see it go when it was simply wrong for *Miss Liberty.* Merman found the audience reaction tepid and declared the song was out. Berlin tried again with more appropriate subject matter, a ponderous song called "Free," but the results were no better. ("Free" would be reworked as "Snow" for the film *White Christmas.*)

"You're Just in Love," a trademark Berlin counterpoint song, was one of the big hits from the show's score. On Broadway Merman sang it with Russell Nype. In the film adaptation, she sang with Donald O'Connor.

Merman then said she "wanted a number with the kid," referring to Russell Nype, who had unexpectedly made a big hit in the first act with "It's a Lovely Day." His crew cut and horn-rimmed glasses gave the show an up-to-date look. At first Nype had feared he would be let go if Merman felt he was getting more applause than she was. Berlin's first counterpoint song, "Simple Melody," from *Watch Your Step,* was enjoying a revival at that time with a new recording by Bing Crosby and his son Gary. Berlin thought that if he could do something similar, it would solve the problem. In New Haven he worked on the number. On opening night in Boston, Merman and Nype stopped the show in the second act, with Nype listing the reasons he thought he was ill, while Merman sang a counter-melody that dovetailed with Nype's, explaining, "You're Just in Love." The audience called for seven encores that night. Berlin was doubly happy when the song soon made the Hit Parade.

ABOVE: Merman and Paul Lukas, who played Merman's love interest, Cosmo Constantine. Lukas was asked to speak-sing, but offered to quit during rehearsals "so Mr. Berlin can get someone who can sing."

RIGHT: Galina Talva (center), who played Princess Maria, dances "The Ocarina" in the original production of *Call Me Madam.* The role was played by Vera-Ellen in the film version.

Lindsay and Crouse had hoped to update the dialogue throughout the run with references to current political events, as they had done with great success in *State of the Union,* but at the end of the tryouts in Boston, after numerous revi-

sions in both script and song, Merman informed them that she was "Miss Birds Eye of 1950. Not one more change. I'm frozen."

Expectations were running high for the show. Crouse suggested on the eve of its Boston opening that the public seemed to be expecting too much of the new musical comedy. "They seem to think it is going to be another *South Pacific*—with elephants added! It isn't. It's just a good show." But this time the expectations were met: The critics loved the show. The *Times*'s Brooks Atkinson had only a year earlier deemed Berlin "old-fashioned" in reviews of *Miss Liberty.* Now he celebrated the latest triumph in Berlin's career, saying that "his longevity as a composer is not only amazing but gratifying." Berlin took it in stride. "For the first time I got a good notice from Brooks Atkinson," said Berlin, who was critical of the reviewers who said that Merman was great, but were less than enthusiastic about the book of *Call Me Madam.* "This I can't understand because if she's so good, she certainly didn't make it up as she went along."

Among the first-nighters was General Dwight Eisenhower, who played his own part in the production. At the time he was president of Columbia University,

"I love to write songs for Ethel," said Berlin. "I guess it's a little like a dress designer getting an extra kick when he dreams up a gown for a beautiful woman with a perfect figure." Lindsay and Crouse, Merman and Berlin celebrate the success of *Call Me Madam.*

Berlin might jot down lyrics on any paper available. He scribbled the lyrics to "The Hostess with the Mostes' on the Ball" on an office notepad. Perle Mesta liked the phrase so much that she asked permission from Berlin to describe herself that way. Mesta would later say in an interview, "I only hope that someday I become as great a diplomat as Ethel Merman is an actress." Here Merman gets senators from both parties together in "Washington Square Dance."

and disclaimed any interest in national politics, although both parties were court-ing him as a presidential nominee. Berlin admired Eisenhower, and it was the gen-eral who had recommended that *This Is the Army* travel to combat areas where the troops were during World War II. Berlin claimed that he had written a song for Eisenhower in 1948 when there was talk of a run, but then put it away. As he worked on *Call Me Madam,* he saw a spot for a comedy song, and as the show satirized everybody in politics, he adapted the song for the setting. "They Like Ike" was sung by three senators led by Pat Harrington. If Eisenhower did run, he now had a campaign song. When the general was nominated as the Republican candidate for the presidency in 1952, as Berlin had predicted in the show, Berlin adapted the song to simply "I Like Ike," a slogan that was one of the most successful and memorable in American political history, even if the song itself is only dimly remembered. Berlin revised the lyrics in the show as Eisenhower's status changed.

After *Call Me Madam,* Berlin briefly considered working with Abbott again on the musical version of *A Tree Grows in Brooklyn.* He also wrote and rewrote a number of songs for a show variously titled *Wise Guy, The Mizner Story,* and *Senti-mental Guy,* about Addison and Wilson Mizner, two con-man brothers during the first quarter of the twentieth century. Addison became an architect, developing the Palm Beach style, and is credited with establishing the city of Boca Raton. Wilson, who had been a friend of Berlin's from his early days, never really gave up the con. He was also a playwright, but his legacy today is the expression "never give a sucker an even break." Berlin had dedicated some of his early songs "to my pal Wilson Mizner," and he was eager to work on the show with George S. Kaufman and S. N. Behrman, who were working on the book. Berlin approached Merman about the show, but she decided to take time off to be with her new husband, and bit by bit the show fell apart, despite several interesting songs by Berlin. Four decades later, Stephen Sondheim would wrestle with the same material, and despite several productions in regional theaters, the show never reached Broadway.

Berlin worked on several songs for a *Music Box Revue* television spectacular in 1957 that was to have starred Mary Martin, Perry Como, and George Gobel, but again, the show died on the vine. He took up painting, but decided that "as a painter, I'm a pretty good songwriter." He tried to retire, but was too restless. He had worked for nearly sixty years, and idleness made him nervous. As he told one journalist in July of 1962, "I went up to the country, thinking this is the thing to do. Then I found out the trouble about retiring is that you've got to retire to something else—to a hobby—which I didn't have.... I had at least a dozen offers to get involved with shows—and several turned out to be very big hits. But the projects didn't interest me. I was afraid to go to bat ... when I finally decided I was going to dip my toe into the cold water again, I called up [Leland] Hayward and said I

Berlin at his country home in the Catskills during his hiatus between *Call Me Madam* and *Mr. President.*

wanted to do a show with Lindsay and Crouse. I had worked with them only on *Madam* and it was a helluva hit." In the years after *Call Me Madam,* Berlin had suffered from chronic physical ailments and had become depressed. In contrast, songwriting made him happy. He concluded the interview, saying he could do away with doctors and medicine because "when you are busy at something that is a part of you, you forget about yourself."

That "something" was a new Broadway show about a popular president who is getting ready to leave the White House, *Mr. President.* The trio worked on the script and songs by mail, as they had on *Call Me Madam,* when Berlin had gone to Nassau to work on the score. Berlin wrote the biggest, but unfortunately not the best, score of his career: nineteen songs without one hit or truly memorable tune among them. He also resorted to a mawkish patriotic finale "This Is a Great Country," that fit his definition two decades earlier of "an audience trap," where theatergoers have no choice but to clap for a flag waved in the second act.

Of course the public did not yet know this, and the advance for the show at the time was the largest in Broadway history: $2.5 million. The tryouts in Boston received the worst notices of any show Berlin had ever worked on. By calling some of Berlin's songs "corny," the reviewers

VARIETY

PRICE 35¢

Published Weekly at 154 West 46th Street, New York 36, N. Y., by Variety, Inc. Annual subscription, $15. Single copies, 35 cents.
Second Class Postage at New York, N. Y.
© COPYRIGHT 1962 BY VARIETY, INC. ALL RIGHTS RESERVED

64 PAGES

NEW YORK, WEDNESDAY, JULY 18, 1962

Vol. 227 No. 8

BERLIN'S B'WAY BOUNCE-BACK

ABOVE: The show business' bible, *Variety*, announced Berlin's return to Broadway in 1962 with *Mr. President*.

RIGHT: *Look* magazine assigned Henri Cartier-Bresson to photograph Berlin during the rehearsals and tryouts. In Boston (left to right), director Josh Logan, Berlin, Lindsay and Crouse, and producer Leland Hayward.

BELOW: The First Family enjoys a happy moment on stage in *Mr. President*. From left: Nanette Fabray, Robert Ryan, Anita Gillette, and Jerry Strickler.

spared him the worst of the criticism. Ever the optimist, Berlin saw the bad reviews as a potentially good thing for the show. "Instead of the built-in resentment that any big pre-sold show is bound to run into, [the audience] may be willing to come and judge it on our merits." He already accepted that critics would not like it. "Maybe I shouldn't say this. Maybe my colleagues wouldn't agree with me. But speaking for myself, I don't think we have a Pulitzer Prize show, a Critics Circle Award show. I do think that we have a show that audiences will love." With a weak book and score there was no easy fix. As one review put it, "You can't say nothing happens in *Mr. President*. Unfortunately, not much of it seems to matter very much."

Director Josh Logan, who had a fair number of hits to his credit, reasoned that the critics did not like *Mr. President* because "there's nothing avant-garde about this show... somebody said we should call it the *Hardy Family in the White House* and there's some truth in that. This is a very simple, nostalgic story, almost a fairy tale—you could call it *Just Suppose*." But Russel Crouse knew *Mr. President* did not live up even to their own expectations, saying that, "The one thing certain is that the audiences so far have liked it better than we do. By the time we get to New York, we may even like it ourselves." It did make

Robert Ryan and Nanette Fabray played
President Stephen Decatur Henderson and
his wife, Nell.

it to Broadway, but its record advance ticket sales kept it open for only eight
months.

Mr. President was not only Berlin's last show, it was Lindsay and Crouse's as
well. Logan went on to direct a few more flops; more than a decade later, Hayward
also produced two more shows, and they too were flops. For all of these men, their
day on Broadway had passed. They were all masters of a type of entertainment that
was no longer in vogue. All were younger than Berlin, but all suffered the same fate.

These men liked to entertain, and sometimes made an audience think. They
hoped audiences would leave the theater humming a good song. Critics and audiences by the early sixties were looking for theater that was more complex and less
conventional. Berlin did write one more hit for Broadway, but even its title had the
word "old-fashioned" in it.

Berlin's final years were quiet ones. In his last quarter century, he wrote new songs but he published only two of them. He realized his era of songwriting was over. "It was as if I owned a store," he told music scholar Robert Kimball, "and people no longer wanted to buy what I had to sell." They may not have wanted new songs, but the old songs—"White Christmas," "Easter Parade," "God Bless America," and "Puttin' on the Ritz," among others—continued to sell and were now part of people's lives. He had achieved the dream he set out in 1930's "Let Me Sing and I'm Happy":

What care I who makes the laws of a nation;
Let those who will take care of its rights and wrongs,
What care I who cares
For the world's affairs
As long I can sing its popular songs.

Over an extraordinary career, Berlin published more than eight hundred songs, and his files included more than four hundred others. The joy he had in writing the songs had grown exponentially in the generations who now sang the songs. Irving Berlin's songs joined apple pie and mother on the list of things quintessentially American.

Berlin at home during his last photo session on the afternoon of September 5, 1974. Photograph by Jill Krementz.

AMERICA
1954-1989

The Song Is Ended (but the Melody Lingers On)

1954–1963

1966

1968–1969

1973

1954 Eisenhower awards Berlin a special Presidential Medal "for his services in composing many patriotic songs including 'God Bless America.' "

1963 Berlin begins work on his final film project, *Say It with Music*.

September 21 *Annie Get Your Gun* is revived for a limited run at the New York State Theatre and on ABC television. Ethel Merman returns as Annie Oakley. The production is nominated for two Tonys, for Choreography and Direction.

1968 May 11 Ed Sullivan hosts a ninety-minute television tribute to Berlin on his eightieth birthday (above).

1969 April *Say It with Music* is canceled by MGM.

May 6 At a White House dinner honoring returning POWs from Vietnam, Berlin sings "God Bless America" with President Richard Nixon. It is his last public appearance.

1977–1982

1986

1988

1989

1977 Berlin is awarded the Medal of Freedom by President Gerald Ford.

1982 Dutch recording artist Taco scores a hit with a disco-flavored "Puttin' on the Ritz."

July 4 At the one-hundredth-anniversary celebration of the Statue of Liberty, twelve naturalized citizens receive the Liberty Medal from President Ronald Reagan. Berlin is one of the recipients but does not attend the ceremony.

May 11 Centennial birthday celebration by ASCAP at Carnegie Hall featuring Frank Sinatra, Tommy Tune, Leonard Bernstein, and many others (above).

July 29 Ellin Berlin dies.

February 26 Berlin's "Mr. Monotony" is finally performed on Broadway in *Jerome Robbins' Broadway*.

September 22 Berlin dies in his sleep at his house on Beekman Place, New York City.

Berlin in 1956 surrounded by Boy Scouts after receiving their Silver
Beaver Award for creating the "God Bless America Fund."

SAY IT WITH MUSIC

"It's just a fad," said Berlin in 1958 when asked about the latest trend in popular music: rock and roll. "It's rather hard on the ears and the sensibilities, but we have had novelty periods before. They come to an end and melody always wins out." To another reporter he declared, "Rock-and-roll music has lasted longer than I expected. But it will eventually die out, as did ragtime, swing, and other temporary successes." At seventy, Berlin was simply too old to rock and roll. The shift in public taste, and the way music would be made for the next half-century would finally cause him to retire.

On Broadway, the integrated musical came into its own. Composers thought of the show as a whole, not simply how many hits were in it. Berlin was dismissive. "When they don't have a hit they call them integrated. I believe in hits." Berlin did see his music as an art form, explaining, "It's just as important to write a hit song as it is to paint a beautiful picture." But he said of himself, "I'm not a composer. I'm a songwriter. That's all I ever was. It's all I ever wanted to be."

For the songwriter, it was simple: "In the final analysis, it's the people—not thinking as individuals but en masse—who make it a hit, and they can't be wrong. You know, sometimes some writers get so expert in their jobs, they get a little too good. They write oblique songs. They're embarrassed to say 'I love you,' or to mention mother or to say 'God Bless America.' But the public isn't embarrassed at all. These things are universal. Everybody falls in love. Everybody hates to get up in the morning. Everybody loves America." He felt that *My Fair Lady* was the best musical of his lifetime and went to see it three times, yet he felt the emphasis on the libretto of a show was overrated. "Did they need a book of *My Fair Lady* to write 'I Could Have Danced All Night'? It could have been a dame coming home from a night club." He saw it as a simple Cinderella story, concluding, "You don't have to be different, you don't have to be fresh. You have to be good."

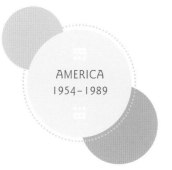

Hirschfeld painted Berlin on the occasion of the songwriter's hundredth birthday in 1988.

Berlin evoking the minstrel show in an undated photograph.

Two American icons intersected when Grandma Moses translated "White Christmas" into a painting, which Berlin acquired. In 1991 the song was published with the painting on the cover.

After the critical failure of *Mr. President,* Berlin turned to Hollywood to create another hit. With Arthur Freed at MGM he conceived a twenty-five-song cavalcade of his greatest hits, *Say It with Music.* He wrote seven new songs specifically for the film. Freed was excited by the prospect and suggested that it be a Berlin biography, but, as always, Berlin rejected the idea.

The cavalcade was announced in June 1963, with Freed producing, Vincente Minnelli directing, and Arthur Laurents writing the script. The cast included Frank Sinatra, Fred Astaire, Judy Garland, Ethel Merman, Pat Boone, and Connie Francis. Only three months earlier, Hollywood had acknowledged Berlin's remarkable talent in a star-studded dinner for the Screen Producer's Guild Milestone Award. On the dais with Berlin at the Beverly Hills Hilton were many of the men and women

who had played prominent roles in his film career, including Sam Goldwyn, Darryl Zanuck, Fred Astaire, Arthur Freed, and Bob Hope. After five hours of testimonials, jokes, and songs, Berlin sat down at a piano and led the thousand-plus crowd in "God Bless America." Over the next six years there would be various cast changes, and replacements within the creative team of *Say It with Music*. Just when it looked as though it would go into production, MGM was sold and its new owners killed the project. Berlin was furious, but there was little he could do. "If Louis B. Mayer had been the head of Metro," he dictated to his secretary for a statement that he never sent out, "*Say It with Music* would have been made, released, and piled up a large profit for MGM."

ABOVE: Berlin is surrounded by stars at the Screen Producers' Guild Milestone Award in 1963. Left to right: George Jessel, Rosalind Russell, Groucho Marx, Frank Sinatra, Irving Berlin, Dinah Shore, Dean Martin, and Danny Kaye.

BELOW: Ethel Merman reprises the title role in *Annie Get Your Gun* in 1966.

At seventy-eight he wrote his last show-stopper, "An Old-Fashioned Wedding," for the 1966 revival of *Annie Get Your Gun*. Berlin suggested to producer Richard Rodgers that the secondary romance of the show, "the dull stuff," be dropped. He felt that the story was necessary in the forties, but that now it was superfluous. To make up for the two songs that were cut along with the story line, Berlin came up with his last counterpoint song, in which Frank extols the virtue of a "simple wedding" while Annie, played again by Ethel Merman, sings about "a wedding like the Vanderbilts have." Berlin said, "I always like to write songs that come out of a dramatic situation."

The production was a rousing success, and it was the only Broadway revival he would ever see of his work. Its triumph got him thinking about other ventures. He talked

Ellin and Irving Berlin in the autumn of 1969.

about a new *Music Box Revue* and a musical about life on the Lower East Side. Writing came easier to him now because "I recognize the wrong choices quicker." He even tried to sell a remake of the film of *Annie Get Your Gun* to Darryl Zanuck, with Barbra Streisand in the lead.

But he knew his working days were over. When asked if he would retire, he responded, "Here's all I can tell you about that—someday I expect people to say 'Berlin's slipping... He's falling... He fell... No, he's dead!' " But he knew that he, and the contemporaries who were friends, rivals, and collaborators, were viewed as "antiques, museum pieces." Unlike many of the songwriters of his generation, he owned the copyrights to his work, and as the years went on, he guarded them closely, and sometimes bitterly. According to Berlin, a Japanese consortium had tried to buy his publishing rights for an incredible sum, but he said he wouldn't know what to do with the money, and they wouldn't know what to do with the songs.

Although the American public turned to new music, he still felt strongly about the country. "Who has the right to love this country more than I do?" he asked in 1968 at eighty. "I don't forget where and how I started. If America were a company, I'd buy all the stock I could get, put it away. It's the greatest land in the world."

He was devoted to Ellin and his growing family, and when he felt well, he wrote songs for his grandchildren. After visiting the White House to welcome home returning POWs from Vietnam in 1973, he never made another public appearance. He maintained contact with the world by phone, calling his office several times a day to check on business, and keeping in touch with a small circle of friends and admirers, those who, he felt, understood his work.

If he was the rare writer who owned his copyrights, he was virtually alone in being among the writers who outlived some of them. For a sharp businessman like Berlin it must have been tough to see his early songs, especially "Alexander's Ragtime Band," move into the public domain.

In a sense that is where they have always been. The public embraced his music early on and never let it go. For generations of Americans, Berlin supplied the soundtrack to their lives. His songs are so much a part of American culture that it hardly seems possible they were written by any one person or so recently. Songs like "God Bless America," "White Christmas," "Always," "Anything You Can Do," and "Puttin' on the Ritz" are a part of the national consciousness, and most people sing them without any idea of who wrote them. Although Berlin died on

In the week after Berlin's death in 1989, Edward Sorel imagined Berlin's arrival in heaven, where he is welcomed by Bach, Schubert, Mozart, and his old friend George Gershwin. Richard Wagner, at the lower left, sulks at the arrival of yet another Jew.

September 22, 1989, his songs continue to give testimony to his talents, whether written for Broadway, Hollywood, or America.

> So what can a songwriter say?
> What can a songwriter do?
> A fiddler can speak with his fiddle,
> A singer can speak with his voice,
> An actor can speak
> With his tongue in his cheek,
> But a songwriter has no choice.
> Whatever ever his rights or his wrongs,
> He can only speak with his songs.

EPILOGUE

For one who died in 1989, Irving Berlin has been surprisingly busy on Broadway, in Hollywood, and all across America. His connection with the public has grown stronger in recent years with revivals, rediscoveries, and even premieres of his words and music.

On and off Broadway, Berlin seems never to have left the stage. In 1995 a concert production of *Call Me Madam* defined the importance of the *Encore!* series at New York's City Center, and helped establish it as the best opportunity to reacquaint an audience with musicals of the past. Tyne Daly's riveting performance demonstrated how the show transcended even the legendary Ethel Merman.

The following year, *Louisiana Purchase* was presented in concert format at Carnegie Weill Recital Hall to great acclaim, and the subsequent recording provided the cast album that Berlin had always wished had been made. At the same time, Off-Broadway was laughing with a revival of *The Cocoanuts.* Without the chaos of the real-life Marx Brothers (but with actors playing them), critics and audiences once again appreciated the show's tuneful score and George Kaufman's very funny book.

The 1998 Off-Broadway revival of *As Thousands Cheer* proved, as Michael Feingold wrote in *The Village Voice,* that "nothing's changed in America's consciousness except the names and the more explicit sexual details." He concluded by observing, "They don't write songs like that any more. Dammit." Here they stop the presses for the opening number, "Man Bites Dog."

In 1998 *As Thousands Cheer* was presented Off-Broadway in strikingly simple fashion. "Topical satire, especially the kind found in musical revues, tends to age about as well as sushi," observed *New York Times* critic Ben Brantley. "The surprise of this winningly modest presentation of a vintage hit is that it shows no sign at all of spoilage. The comic bite in Hart's lines and in Berlin's lyrics still clicks crisply, and the work's portrait of the pandering ways of celebrities and the journalists who cover them remains spot on."

In 1999 Berlin was back on Broadway with a hit *Annie Get Your Gun,* starring Bernadette Peters. Just as Berlin and Dorothy Fields had done three decades earlier, the producers revised the show once again. The secondary love story was restored, "An Old-Fashioned Wedding" was retained, and the expert writer Peter Stone was brought in to rewrite the book. Stone walked the fine line between political correctness and contemporary sensibility by setting the whole production as part of Buffalo Bill's Wild West Show. "The Native Americans in Buffalo Bill's show are now quite obviously playing along with the gag," wrote *Time*'s Richard Zoglin. "In a musical that proclaims, 'There's no people like show people,' why not?" Two years into the run, Peters, the reigning queen of Broadway, was replaced by a newcomer, Reba McEntire, a country-and-western performer, who seemed born to the role. "Someone said, 'I didn't know Irving Berlin wrote country songs!,'" McEntire told *Billboard*. "But they certainly fit me to a 'T.' They're timeless, marvelous, funny, intriguing, and a pleasure and an honor to sing every night with my Oklahoma twang and all!"

Annie Get Your Gun was the appropriate vehicle for Berlin to return to Broadway. Soon after his death his estate had joined forces with the organization founded by the show's original producers, Rodgers and Hammerstein. The organization's representation of Berlin's music worldwide has been wildly successful.

In 2004 director and choreographer Susan Stroman took fourteen Berlin songs to create *The Blue Necklace* ballet for the New York City Ballet as the first half of an evening-length double bill titled *Double Feature.* Stroman told a melodramatic tale of a young woman forced to leave her foundling baby on the church steps in an homage to silent film.

Berlin has also remained a constant presence in Hollywood. More than thirty films since 1989 have featured his songs in small and yet significant ways. One of the enduring images of late-twentieth-century popular filmmaking is of Macaulay Culkin mimicking the Drifters' version of "White Christmas" in *Home Alone* (1990). After Berlin famously turned down Steven Spielberg's 1988 request to use "Always" in his film of the same name because the songwriter was saving it for something he was working on, the director did include "Cheek to Cheek" in *Artificial Intelligence: AI.* The same song was included in *The English Patient* (1996) and many other films. Even documentaries—for example, "I Want to Go Back to Michigan," in *Bowling for Columbine* (2002)—have used Berlin compositions.

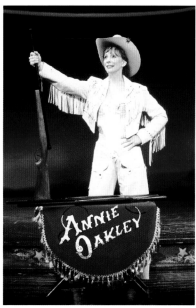

The reigning queen of the Broadway musical, Bernadette Peters (top), took on the daunting task of filling Ethel Merman's shoes for the 1999 revival of *Annie Get Your Gun.* Country-and-western singer Reba McEntire (bottom) had an equal challenge filling Peters's cowboy boots when she made her Broadway debut later in the run. Both hit a bull's-eye with critics and audiences.

A holiday tradition was born in 2004 when the film of *White Christmas* was adapted for the stage. Appropriately, eighty-eight years after "I Love a Piano" was introduced on stage, it became a show-stopping number once again (opposite) in the "new" musical.

"Blue Skies," Berlin's first film song, continues to appear in movies from the independent *Romeo Must Die* (2000) to the major studio *Star Trek: Nemesis* (2002). Many of the Berlin songs written originally for Fred Astaire have become cinematic shorthand for style and class. Berlin also proved to be prescient when refusing to participate in any screen biography of himself. Cole Porter suffered a second screen biopic (even less successful than the first), *De-Lovely,* in 2004, in which an actor attempted to portray Berlin.

Three films in the 2004 holiday season continued the tradition of including "White Christmas" in their sound-tracks. More significantly the song continues to be recorded by a wide variety of performers in the twenty-first century, from Kenny Rogers to Kenny Loggins, and from Mannheim Steamroller to The Flaming Lips, making it the most recorded song of all time. Bing Crosby's original recording has sold over a hundred million copies, making it the best-selling record in history, according to the *Guinness Book of World Records.* The Irving Berlin Music Company still sells over fifteen thousand copies of the sheet music every year. The song inspired a book-long meditation, *White Christmas: The Story of an American Song,* by Jody Rosen, who used it as a prism to view Berlin's career.

In 2004 the film *White Christmas* became a stage musical. Taking the storyline and almost all of the songs from the film and adding a few choice Berlin gems from the catalogue, the producers gave a whole new life to one of the holiday's most popular films. The new musical opened in San Francisco in the fall of 2004 and, as of this writing, seems poised to join the short list of holiday musicals per-formed coast to coast.

Shows and films have helped to spread Berlin's work across the country, but the interest in his music has never waned. Baby-boomers rediscovered the songs of their parents' era and a new audience was formed around both old and new recordings, such as *Unsung Berlin,* which included a variety of performers singing unpublished or little-known Berlin songs.

When America needed Berlin the most, his work was there to assuage a shaken nation after the terrorist attacks of 2001. On the afternoon of September 11, every member of Congress gathered on the steps of the Capitol to assure citizens that America would respond. Spontaneously, someone began to sing "God Bless America," and everyone there joined in. The scene was repeated when Wall Street re-opened and thereafter at baseball games and Broadway curtain calls. In the *Wall Street Journal* Terry Teachout asked rhetorically, "What makes us turn as if by instinct to 'God Bless America' in times of trial?" Berlin's second daughter, Linda Emmet, told a reporter, " 'God Bless America' evokes a sense of unity and calm: 'Stand beside her and guide her through the night with a light from above.' What happened on September 11 could metaphorically be the night; the light could be our continuing to move on."

A year after the attacks, Berlin's visual legacy continued to permeate our culture when he was honored with a U.S. postage stamp with the words of "God Bless America" behind his portrait. The stamp was unveiled during the "Broadway on Broadway" celebration in Times Square as more than fifty thousand people sang the unofficial national anthem.

In late 2001 *The Complete Lyrics of Irving Berlin* was published, edited by music scholar Robert Kimball and Linda Emmet. As the nation once again found both solace and strength in Berlin's words, readers were reminded that he had supplied the songs for every occasion. "As much as we think we may know Berlin through his perennials that seem to stand above and apart from their times, *The Complete Lyrics of Irving Berlin* tells a different story," Stephen Holden wrote in the *New York Times.* "The anthology finds Berlin as deeply engaged with his times as any of his songwriting peers, and it can almost be perused as the public diary of one man's engagement with American culture over more than half a century." Another critic compared the book to "reading one long epic poem, mapping the contours of the American century in metric form." The breadth of Berlin's work means that we will always be reacquainting ourselves with his songs.

The century since Berlin wrote his first song would simply not be the same without his contributions. In spring 1994 Charles Osgood, host of *CBS Sunday Morning,* reflected on the "Wall to Wall Irving Berlin" that New York's Symphony Space had presented a few weeks earlier. "Tell the truth, it seemed a little mad, didn't it?," he remarked. "A twelve-hour marathon of music by one man.... Does it seem mad now? Think of a year in this country, from ragtime to our time, think of a song. Who wrote that song you are thinking of?"

ACKNOWLEDGMENTS

My work on this book has been aided by the kindnesses of many people. The Berlin family—Mary Ellin and Marvin Barrett, Linda and Edouard Emmet, and Elizabeth Peters, who opened their homes to me—have been exceedingly generous, and I have benefited greatly from their insights throughout my research and writing. In addition, the remarkable staff of The Rodgers & Hammerstein Organization, which represents the Estate of Irving Berlin, has been unstinting with its time, efforts, and good humor, all of which have made my job so much easier. I extend special thanks there to Bert Fink, Carol Cornicelli, and Ted Chapin. I am also grateful to Harriet Whelchel, managing editor at Harry N. Abrams, Inc., who first proposed that I write the book. Her guidance and friendship throughout the project have been a balm and tonic. My editor, Elaine Stainton, turned the potentially ulcer-producing process of seeing the book through production into an efficient and positive one; and I owe an extra low bow of admiration to designer Laura Lindgren, who took my straw and turned it into gold.

My work would have been difficult, if not impossible, without the help of the following people: Amy Asch, Jean Ashton, Tom Barrick, Jane Batt, Jerry Beck, Stacey Behlmer, Margaret L. Berg, Randl Bye, John Cahoon, Scott Candiotti, Anne Coco, Douglas Colby, Tara Craig, Robert Cushman, Jacqueline Davis and the staff and librarians at the New York Public Library for the Performing Arts, Helen Demeestere, Mary Dickens, Maxine Fleckner Ducey, Eric Evans, Phillip Furia, Laurie Geissel, Madeline Gibson, Bill Goldstein, Jennifer Greenberg, Barbara Hall, Malinda Hartsig, Eric Himmel, Louise Kerz Hirschfeld, Dorinda Hoffman, Mark Horowitz, Marty Jacobs, Ann Kaplan, Christine Karatnytsky, Mark Klausen, Kristine Krueger, Marguerite Lavin, Bruce Lawton, Lucia and Pierre Lebvere, Jennifer Lee, Joan and Sandy Leopold, John Leopold, Henry Leopold, David and Arlene LeVine, Ann Liebgold, Jeremy Megraw, Linda Harris Mehr and the staff and librarians at the Herrick Library at the Academy of Motion Pictures Arts and Sciences, Hugh Munro Neely, Stuart and Amy Ng, Karen Nickeson, Diane Nilsen, Debbie Oliver, Florence Palomo, Tom Pearson, Barbara Cohen Stratnyer, Bob Taylor, Dace Traube, Elisa Urbanelli, Ray White and the librarians of the Performing Arts Reading Room at the Library of Congress, Sheepie and Chipper, and Marian Young. As always, the love and support of my wife, Laura Rathgeb, has seen me through.

INDEX

CREDITS

Illustrations located by page and position: t=top; b=bottom; l=left; r=right; ul=upper left; ur=upper right; uc=upper center; ll= lower left; lr = lower right; lc= lower center; cr= center right; cl=center left; bkgr=background

Courtesy of the Academy of Motion Picture Arts and Sciences: 3, 5r, 76–77, 85, 116–117, 121, 123 (both), 126 (both), 127ul, 128b, 130, 133ur, 136b, 138ur, 200; Courtesy of the Academy of Motion Picture Arts and Sciences and Warner Entertainment: 126ur; Illustration reprinted by permission of the Estate of Peter Arno: 106ur; Author's collection: 2 2nd ul, 2 3rd ul, 4, 10ur, 10ll, 10lr, 13, 14l; 37t, 38l, 39ur, 64t, 78ul, 78lr, 86ul, 105ur, 122ur, 128ur, 156ul, 178l, 179b, 195 (both), 197, 198lr, 204–05, 214ul; Used by Permission of the Estate of Irving Berlin: 2lr, 10 (except ur, ll, lr), 11 (all), 15ll, 16b, 18ll, 19 (all), 20, 21 (both), 24l, 25 (both), 28r, 29 (both), 38 ur, 39b, 40–41, 42 (except lc), 43 (except b), 44, 45, 46b, 47, 48b, 49 (both), 50, 51, 54 (ur), 55 (except lr), 62, 63, 66r, 68ul, 68ur, 69ur, 70 (except ll), 72b, 73 (both), 75, 78 (except ul, lr), 79 (except ul), 80, 82lr, 84lr, 86r, 94 (except ul, b), 95 (except uc), 98, 101ur, 107, 108b, 109, 113, 118 (all), 119 (except b), 135 (both), 142–43, 144ul, 144ur, 144ll, 149, 150–51, 152 (except t), 153 (both), 154ll, 155t, 156b, 157l, 158 (except ur), 159, 161ur, 161ll, 162b), 163 (both), 164–65, 166 (except uc, lc), 176cr, 180 (both), 181ll, 182ul, 185, 188–89 (all), 190, 192 (both), 194, 199b, 202ul, 203 (both), 210r, 211l, 215ur, 219, 220ll, 224 (except lr), 225, 227, 228, 229 (both), 230, 233ur; Used by Permission of the Estate of Irving Berlin. Courtesy of the Irving Berlin Collection, Music Division, Library of Congress: 16t, 18ul, 22 (both), 23 (both), 24r, 34ul, 46t, 48t, 66l, 70ll, 71t, 94ul, 95uc, 106ul, 140ul, 144 3rd ul, 146, 158ur, 160, 162ul, 178ll, 179ur, 196l, 199ur, 218ul; Photograph by Mathieu Bourgois: 70ul, 101ur, 158ul, 224ul; Brown Brothers, Sterling, PA: 14r; 33ul; Joseph Urban Papers, Rare Book and Manuscript Library, Columbia University: 4–5, 52–53, 58lr, 59t; Cecil Beaton/Vanity Fair © 1930 Condé Nast Publications Inc.: 72lr; © Corbis. All Rights Reserved: 17, 112b, 152t; Photograph by Louise Dahl-Wolfe. © 1989 Center for Creative Photography, Arizona Board of Regents, Louise Dahl-Wolfe Archive: 217; Photo by Eileen Darby/Time & Life Pictures/Getty Images: 173; Helen Dryden/Vanity Fair © Condé Nast Publications Inc.: 37ll; Photo by Eliot Elisofon/Time & Life Pictures/Getty Images: 216 (both);

Photo by Rex Hardy Jr./Time Life Pictures/Getty Images: 136t; Melvin R. Seiden Collection, The Harvard Theatre Collection, The Houghton Library: 116; Hershenson/Allen Archive: 83; © The Al Hirschfeld Foundation. Reproduced by arrangement with The Margo Feiden Galleries: 88, 169, 174ul, 201ur, 214ul; Hulton Archive/Getty Images: 129ur; Courtesy of the University of Illinois Library at Urbana-Champaign: 184 (all); Photo by George Karger/Pix Inc./Time & Life Pictures/Getty Images: 168, 182ll; Collection of Anne Kaufman Schneider. © The Ben Solowey Collection: 84ul; Photograph © Jill Krementz. Photo taken September 5 1974. Courtesy of Jill Krementz: 222–23; Photo by Gene Lester/Getty Images: 186–87, 206; Courtesy of The Seaver Center for Western History Research, Los Angeles County Museum of Natural History: 124 (both), 125 (both); © Joan Marcus. Courtesy of the photographer: 232; Courtesy of MedalofFreedom.com, Part of the Americans.net Family of History and Education Websites: 144lr; Courtesy of Marc Mellon Sculpture Studio, Redding, CT: 147; Illustrated song slide from "Don't You Understand, Honey?" c.1905, slide c.1908, sequence #9, Van Allin Co. Courtesy of the Marnan Collection, Minneapolis, MN: 12; Illustrated song slide from "The Ragtime Soldier Man" 1912, slide c.1912, Scott & Van Allin Co. Courtesy of the Marnan Collection, Minneapolis, MN: 43b; Copyright © 1955 (renewed 1983) Grandma Moses Properties Co., New York: 228; Museum of the City of New York: 8–9, 18ur, 28l, 32ul, 35, 58ll, 61, 64b, 65ur, 65 (all), 74, 97, 99ul, 100, 108ur, 164–65, 166 2nd ll, 171t, 172ll, 176cr, 182ur, 212, 213, 218ur; Jerome Robbins Dance Collection, The New York Public Library for the Performing Arts, Astor, Lenox and Tilden Foundations: 31; Billy Rose Theatre Collection, The New York Public Library for the Performing Arts, Astor, Lenox and Tilden Foundations: 2ul, 30, 32b, 33ul, 33b, 34b, 36, 54ur, 55lr, 56, 59lr, 60, 67, 68b, 69ur, 69b, 71b, 82t, 87t, 89, 90, 91b, 92–93, 94b, 99ur, 101ul, 101ll, 102 (all), 104, 105ll, 106b, 108ul, 110 (all), 111 (both), 112ul, 119b, 120, 122ul, 127lr, 129ul, 131, 132, 133b, 134 (both), 137, 138ll, 138lr, 139, 140ur, 141 (both), 144 2nd ul, 144lc, 145, 154t, 155lr, 157ur, 161lr, 161 inset, 166 2nd ul, 170 (both), 171lr, 172ul, 174b, 175, 176–77 bkgr, 176t, 176ll, 177 (both), 181ur, 182lr, 183 (both), 191, 193, 196lr, 198ul, 202b, 207, 208–209, 210l, 211r, 214b, 221; Courtesy of the Mary Pickford Institute of Film Education: 81; Photo by Robin Platzer/Twin

Images/Time Life Pictures/Getty Images: 224lr; Courtesy of Sardi's: 91ur; © Sevenarts Ltd. Courtesy of AJ Fine Arts: 57; © Edward Sorel. Courtesy of the artist: 231; Edward Steichen/Vanity Fair © 1932 Condé Nast Publications Inc.: 96; Courtesy of Variety: 220ul; Courtesy of Vogue, Condé Nast Archive: 103; Courtesy of Tom Werkman. SoundtrackCollector.com: 87lr; Wisconsin Center for Film and Theater Research: 114 (both), 115.

Lyrics for the songs below are reprinted by permission of Irving Berlin Music Company. Words and music for all songs by Irving Berlin. International copyright secured. All rights reserved.

p. 37: "These are the Costumes the Manager Selected" © Copyright 2001 by The Estate of Irving Berlin; p. 48: "Oh! How I Hate to Get Up in the Morning" © Copyright 1918 Waterson, Berlin &Snyder Co. © Copyright Renewed and assigned to Irving Berlin; p. 51: "Kitchen Police (Poor Little Me)" © Copyright 1918 Irving Berlin. © Copyright Renewed; p. 75: "Russian Lullaby" © Copyright 1927 Irving Berlin. © Copyright Renewed; p. 127: "Let's Face the Music and Dance" © Copyright 1935 Irving Berlin. © Copyright Renewed; p. 131: "He Ain't Got Rhythm" © Copyright 1936 Irving Berlin. © Copyright Renewed; p. 155: "That's What the Well Dressed Man in Harlem Will Wear" © Copyright 1942 Irving Berlin. © Copyright Renewed. Assigned to Winthrop Rutherford, Jr., Anne Phipps Sidamon-Eristoff and Theodore R. Jackson as Trustees of the God Bless America Fund. International Copyright Secured. All Rights Reserved. Used By Permission; p. 155: "This Time (Closing)" © Copyright 1942 Irving Berlin. © Copyright Renewed. Assigned to Winthrop Rutherford, Jr., Anne Phipps Sidamon-Eristoff and Theodore R. Jackson as Trustees of the God Bless America Fund. International Copyright Secured. All Rights Reserved. Used By Permission; p. 161: "Ladies of the Chorus" © Copyright 1942 Irving Berlin. © Copyright Renewed. Assigned to Winthrop Rutherford, Jr., Anne Phipps Sidamon-Eristoff and Theodore R. Jackson as Trustees of the God Bless America Fund. International Copyright Secured. All Rights Reserved. Used By Permission; p. 222: "Let Me Sing and I'm Happy" © Copyright 1928 Irving Berlin Inc. © Copyright Renewed; p. 231: "What Can a Songwriter Say?" © Copyright 2001 by The Estate of Irving Berlin.

The book is dedicated to Eleanor Landis Smahl.

....

Project Manager: Harriet Whelchel
Editor: Elaine Stainton
Designer: Laura Lindgren
Production Manager: Norman Watkins

Library of Congress Cataloging-in-Publication Data
Leopold, David, 1965–
    Irving Berlin's show business : Broadway—Hollywood—America /
by David Leopold.
        p.   cm.
Includes timelines and index.
ISBN 0–8109–5891–0 (hardcover : alk. paper)
1. Berlin, Irving, 1888– 2. Composers—United States—Biography. I. Title.

ML410.B499L46 2005
782.42164'092—dc22   2005002356

Printed and bound in China
10 9 8 7 6 5 4 3 2 1

Harry N. Abrams, Inc.
100 Fifth Avenue
New York, N.Y. 10011
www.abramsbooks.com

Abrams is a subsidiary of